The Paradox of Control in Organizations

This book explores a central paradox of managing in an organization. Business leaders are supposed to be "in control" of the situation in which their businesses find themselves, so if an unexpected event occurs they are supposed to be able to declare that "things are under control." The worst thing that any business leader or manager can do is to declare they are "not in control" of a situation. But how can organizational leaders and managers control matters entirely out of their hands, such as the next action a competitor takes, or the next law a government may pass? Who, or what, is "in control" in an organization? The author attempts to shed light on these questions by exploring his own day-to-day management experiences of life in a large pharmaceutical organization, SmithKline Beecham.

The book is about the dynamic, continually changing formation of patterns of relationships in organizations, through which managers get their work done. Philip J. Streatfield approaches actual management practice from a complexity perspective, understanding organizational life as primarily informal, self-organizing, and transformative in nature. In adopting the perspective of complex responsive processes developed in the first two volumes of this series, the author takes self-organization and emergence as integral themes in his thinking about life in organizations. Conversation is placed at the center of the way humans develop their sense of reality and this book explores, using actual personal experiences, how managers construct their reality in conversation.

The notion that the manager is "in control" does not resonate with experience. In practice, managers find that they have to live with the paradox of being "in control" and "not in control" simultaneously. It is this capacity to live with paradox, the courage to continue to participate creatively in spite of "not being in control," that constitutes effective management.

Philip J. Streatfield is Supply Chain Director at Entertainment UK. Before taking up this position he was Global Medicinals Supply Chain Director at SmithKline Beecham and had spent eighteen years in the pharmaceutical industry involved in managing and improving manufacturing and supply chain activities. He has extensive experience of managing major organizational change.

Complexity and Emergence in Organizations

Series Editors:
Ralph D. Stacey, Douglas Griffin and **Patricia Shaw**
Complexity and Management Centre, University of Hertfordshire

The books in this series each give expression to a particular way of speaking about complexity in organizations. Drawing on insights from the complexity sciences, psychology and sociology, this series aims to develop theories of human organization, including ethics.

Titles in this series:

Complexity and Management
Fad or radical challenge to systems thinking?
Ralph D. Stacey, Douglas Griffin and Patricia Shaw

Complex Responsive Processes in Organizations
Learning and knowledge creation
Ralph D. Stacey

Forthcoming titles in this series include:

Changing the Conversation in Organizations
A complexity approach to change
Patricia Shaw

The Emergence of Leadership
Linking self-organization and ethics
Douglas Griffin

Complexity and Innovation in Organizations
José Fonseca

The Paradox of Control in Organizations

Philip J. Streatfield

London and New York

First published 2001
by Routledge
2 Park Square, Milton Park, Abingdon, Oxon, OX14 4RN

Simultaneously published in the USA and Canada
by Routledge
270 Madison Avenue, New York, NY 10016

Reprinted 2002

Transferred to Digital Printing 2005

Routledge is an imprint of the Taylor & Francis Group

Typeset in Times New Roman by Keystroke, Jacaranda Lodge, Wolverhampton
Printed and bound in Great Britain by Antony Rowe Ltd, Chippenham Wiltshire

British Library Cataloguing in Publication Data
A catalogue record for this book is available from the British Library.

Library of Congress Cataloging in Publication Data
A catalog record for this book has been requested.

ISBN 0–415–25031–5 (hbk)
ISBN 0–415–25032–3 (pbk)

Contents

Series preface
Complexity and Emergence in Organizations

The aim of this series is to give expression to a particular way of speaking about complexity in organizations, one that emphasizes the self-referential, reflexive nature of humans, the essentially responsive and participative nature of human processes of relating and the radical unpredictability of their evolution. It draws on the complexity sciences, which can be brought together with psychology and sociology in many different ways to form a whole spectrum of theories of human organization.

At one end of this spectrum, there is the dominant voice in organization and management theory, which speaks in the language of intention, regularity and control. In this language, managers stand outside the organizational system, which is thought of as an objective, pre-given reality that can be modeled and designed, and they control it. Managers here are concerned with the functional aspects of a system as they search for causal links that promise sophisticated tools for predicting its behavior. The dominant voice talks about the individual as autonomous, self contained, masterful and at the center of an organization. Many complexity theorists talk in a language that is immediately compatible with this dominant voice. They talk about complex adaptive systems as networks of autonomous agents that behave on the basis of regularities extracted from their environments. They talk about complex systems as objective realities that scientists can stand outside of and model. They emphasize the predictable aspects of these systems and see their modeling work as a route to increasing the ability of humans to control complex worlds.

At the other end of the spectrum there are voices from the fringes of organizational theory, complexity sciences, psychology and sociology who are defining a participative perspective. They argue that humans are themselves members of the complex networks that they form and are drawing attention to the impossibility of standing outside of them in order to objectify and model them. With this intersubjective voice people speak as subjects interacting with others in the co-evolution of a jointly constructed reality. These voices emphasize the radically unpredictable aspects of self-organizing processes and their creative potential. These are the voices of decentered agency, which talk about agents and the social world in which they live as mutually created and sustained. This way of thinking weaves together relationship psychologies and the work of complexity theorists who focus on the emergent and radically unpredictable aspects of complex systems. The result is a participative approach to understanding the complexities of organizational life. This series is intended to give expression to the second of these voices defining a participative perspective.

Series editors
Ralph D. Stacey, Douglas Griffin, Patricia Shaw
Complexity and Management Centre,
University of Hertfordshire

Foreword

This is a remarkable and deeply interesting book for those who seek to understand what really happens in organizations as opposed to "what is supposed to happen." The title suggests that the idea of a manager being "in control" in an organization is a paradox and the book effectively demonstrates that this is true. Philip Streatfield effectively demonstrates that managing even the seemingly "scientific production" of a well known cold remedy cannot be "controlled," in that there is a complex process at its heart that is not fully understood, and that the operators use experientially derived implicit knowledge to run it successfully. Using this example he demonstrates the falsity of traditional management views: that a manager is an objective observer standing outside the process, who intentionally designs the processes. These are predictable, and the manager's job is to reduce variability and waste to produce conformity, by detecting and correcting deviations. His own experiences show that successful management required him to be a participant in group interactions in the production process, responding to often unexpected features in the processes and the human interactions as they occur, and making use of diversity rather than attempting to eliminate it. Different examples follow concerning the "real" as opposed to the "rationalized" path to new product development, companies merging, the measurement of performance and supply chain management. They all reinforce the essential revelation of management as participation in a real time, emergent process, of discovery and meaning making, in which although the organization is not "out of control" exactly, managers are not "in control" of what will happen. They are sharing in the discovery of the emerging situation and developing their views and responses, along with other participants, as they go. The experiences serve to illustrate magnificently the new ideas coming from complex systems thinking, where organizations are seen as complex responsive processes, in an emerging situation with multiple views and perspectives, where learning, participating and transforming are the key elements. This book should be read both by would-be managers and those attempting to lay down a conceptual framework for understanding, reflecting upon, and improving the experiences of people in organizations. The experiences recounted in this book, together with the ideas that both underpin and are exemplified by them, mark the beginning of a major revolution in thinking about people, organizations, and society.

Professor Peter Allen
Complex Systems Management Centre
Cranfield School of Management
Cranfield University

Acknowledgments

This book represents the outcome of many conversations and much reflected upon experience throughout my management career to date. It would not have been possible without the interactions I have had with so many people with whom I have worked and enjoyed such great working relationships. I owe much to the team at SK&F Welwyn (particularly Peter Beaumont and Bob White) who gave me my first opportunities in my management career. To many at SmithKline Beecham, particularly John Elliot (thanks for believing in me, John) and Michel Lurquin who helped me to really understand what it means to be people and relationship oriented in the work context. I would also like to thank the supply chain logistics team, especially Carol Skolimowski and David Low, who so valiantly put up with me whilst I mixed trying to make sense of what was happening in the organization with doing the work too!

The inspiration behind this exploration was someone who I now regard as a great friend and colleague, Ralph Stacey. (Having lived through much of this blow-by-blow he has got to be!). Through the work with the doctoral group at the Complexity and Management Centre at the Business School of the University of Hertfordshire and the excellent debates at the Swiss Cottage pub, Ralph has supported the machinations of a frustrated management practitioner grappling with the question of whether he is really in control of what is happening or not. His contribution in the editing of this volume and the process of integrating theory and practice (particularly in chapter five) has been invaluable. The support of others in the doctoral group has also been invaluable. I'd like to highlight particularly Patricia Shaw, Doug Griffin, Peter Fraser and David Bentley all of whom listened and helped with questions and thoughtful insights. Jill Fairbairns has also been a steadfast supporter and indeed suggested that I get back in touch with Ralph in 1994. Thanks Jill.

The support of my family has also been incredibly important in this venture. My wife, Judy, has been a saint in putting up with me working, writing and struggling to be a husband all at once. My two sons Michael and Nicholas have both been great in dealing with a somewhat absent father.

Finally, the major reason I have dedicated time and effort to this work is as a testimony to the efforts of my fellow managers, work colleagues and organizational leaders who, in my view, struggle courageously with the challenge of managing organizations and the paradox of control. Hopefully some of the insights in this work may shed a little more light on what management practitioners really do and what we really have to cope with!

1 Introduction

- The central question for organizations: who is "in control"?
- Real life management: making it up as we go along
- Outline of the book

This book explores management praxis, that is, the art of acting in an organizational context in order to change that context, changing personally in the process. My central concern is to explore how accounting for and reflecting upon my management experience may help other practicing managers to make sense of their own experience. In my search for accounts and explanations of actual management experience, I have encountered two approaches. On the one hand, there are subjective accounts taking the form of biographies and autobiographies of masterful, charismatic leaders and entrepreneurs (for example, Grove, 1996; Tichy and Sherman, 1995). These are stories about the actual experience of successful business leaders who realize visions and fulfill the ambitions of their companies, getting it "right" in a rather rational, orderly way. On the other hand, academic researchers report on management practice, taking the position of objective observers, interviewing, questioning and tape recording conversations with managers. Some adopt a descriptive approach and point to the piecemeal nature of actual management practice (Mintzberg, 1973). They talk about the co-existence of both deliberate and emergent strategies (Mintzberg and Waters, 1985). Others describe the messiness of management practice, labeling it "muddling through" (Lindblom, 1959) or "garbage can" decision making (March and Olsen, 1976). Mostly, however, writers on management are more concerned with prescribing what ought to happen rather than describing what actually does. The more conscientious of these observe what managers are doing, analyze their observations and then produce propositions and hypotheses to be tested in the work environment, as potential prescriptions for success. These prescriptions are invariably a sequence of rational steps to do with measuring, planning and monitoring, which are supposed to enable the manager to stay "in control."

A key question for me is whether any of these approaches yield insights that assist managers to make sense of the sometimes painful experiences in the actual messiness of ordinary, daily life in organizations. That question arose for me, in a particularly acute form in 1989, when the company I worked for, SmithKline Beckman (SKB), was widely reported to be failing to deliver the results required by its shareholders and so merged with another company to form a new organization (see chapter three). I found that experience both painful and challenging, as did most of my friends and colleagues. I am sure that none of us wanted to repeat it, although most of us subsequently had to. At the time, I tried to understand why this had happened. I had great respect for the senior executives of the company and their management capabilities, and I had believed that they could steer the business effectively into the future. Surely, there had to be some rational explanation for what had happened and prescriptions for avoiding its recurrence. Surely somebody had been there before and written the prescription for success. If only senior managers at SKB had read the right papers or books, then we should have been able to avoid what had happened. In searching for explanations, I returned to what I had learned on my MBA course a few years earlier. I looked for accounts that described and made sense of experiences similar to mine but found nothing that offered explanations which resonated with my lived experience. Neither the subjective accounts of the successful practitioners, nor the objective, descriptive and prescriptive accounts of the researchers, helped me to make sense of my experience.

My dissatisfaction with what I will call mainstream approaches to making sense of management experience has led me to take my own experience seriously. It is mainly my own experience that I am presenting in this book and now, in reflection, trying to understand. I am trying to present it as I felt it, with all its mess and mixture of success and failure. In doing this, I use a narrative approach, telling the story of my experiences and then reflecting upon them in order to make sense of them. My purpose in undertaking this personally reflective approach is to gain insights that enable me to make more sense of my experience and so improve my praxis. For me, such reflection on personal experience is a more powerful way of getting at the richness of experience as I and others lived it, than that advocated by mainstream approaches. This personal approach does not produce generalizations that can be "applied" by others to their experience. However, my stories and reflections may resonate with the experiences of others and so assist in their sense-making processes.

Why should it be unusual for practicing managers to reflect publicly on the "real" messiness of their own experience? The answer is not difficult to find. Managers are supposed to be successful all of the time and it is rarely acceptable to own up to not knowing or failing. Many of the processes of management are political and involve the pursuit of personal agendas. Adopting a personally reflective approach is, therefore, potentially dangerous in terms of one's further career progression. Nevertheless, I think it is worth taking the risk to convey something of the messy "reality" of management.

The central question for organizations: who is "in control"?

As I came to reflect more and more on my practice as a manager, a key question emerged for me: who, or what is "in control" of an organization? This book is an attempt to shed light on that question by exploring the ordinary experiences of life in a large pharmaceutical manufacturing organization. I will be paying attention to the dynamic nature of the way in which managers construct meaning in their interactions with each other. In this book, I will be arguing for an alternative to mainstream thinking about organizations and their management. This is a perspective in which an organization is thought of as complex responsive processes of relating (Stacey *et al.*, 2000; Stacey, 2001). This perspective provides an understanding of the self-organizing, transformative processes of organizing. In particular, I will be attending to fives themes.

The first theme is that of *dynamic pattern formation*. By pattern I mean coherence or order as "a combination of qualities, acts, tendencies, . . . forming a consistent or characteristic arrangement" (Webster's Dictionary, 1989). Patterns are about relationships, and human relationships are fluid in the sense that they are continually forming and changing. I therefore see them as dynamic and evolving. These patterns of meaning, with which I will primarily be concerned, emerge in our conversations and our actions as members of our organizations.

The second theme is that of *self organization and emergence*. Self organization means that there is no agent doing the overall organizing but rather numerous agents interacting to produce an overall pattern. It is the pattern of meaning that is organizing itself in the bodily interaction of people. Organization is a sense of order, or recognition of patterns, and dynamic processes form those patterns. Self organization and emergence are central themes in the thinking of complexity scientists in fields as diverse as economics (Arthur, 1988), evolutionary biology (Kauffman, 1993), physics (Gell-Mann, 1994) and urban studies (Allen, 1982). The complexity sciences provide analogies for complex responsive processes in human organizations. This theme of self organization introduces the notion that intentions emerge in spontaneously self-organizing interactions.

The third theme follows from the second and has to do with the *qualities of interaction, or relating*. This particular theme reflects an assumption that the development of political, social and cultural order is the collective result of non-linear interactions (Mainzer, 1996).

The fourth theme is that of *anxiety*. The importance of this theme became more and more apparent as I reflected on the relationships and experiences described in this book. There were two major sources that triggered this as an area of interest for me. The first was Stacey (1996) who explores the importance of emotion and living with anxiety for the creative processes in an organization. He extended the work of Isabel Menzies-Lyth whose studies of nursing in a general hospital led her to question how "nurses could tolerate so much anxiety" (Menzies-Lyth, 1988: 45). The exploration of the institutional aspects of living with anxiety in hospitals helped to identify the underlying nature of anxiety in that kind of work and pointed to the importance of exploring the impact of anxiety for organizations and institutions generally.

The fifth theme is that of *conversation* as a self-organizing phenomenon in which meaning emerges. Here the definition of conversation is broad. It incorporates verbal discourse at a surface level and deeply reflective thought, writing and discussion. It covers dialogue, the search for new meaning and the making sense of experience. Conversation may arise spontaneously in the moment, or it can take the form of a slowed down reflective act of reporting, story-telling or writing narratives. When reading a book we are in conversation with the author. When we are interacting with each other, verbally and in the medium of feelings, we are in conversation. When we are reflecting on events and trying to see a pattern in them, we are in conversation with ourselves. Similarly when we write, we are in conversation with ourselves. Shotter places conversation at the center of the way we develop our sense of reality. He argues that "present in the conversational background to our lives are many forms of talk, with their own peculiar properties, currently without a 'voice' in the contests within this sphere. If they were to gain a voice, it could change our lives" (Shotter, 1994: 18). In this book, I attempt to give voice to some of these different forms of talk in the stories about my experience.

For me, these themes illuminate in various ways the central question of whether or not managers in an organization are "in control." As I have already said, this was a question raised in a particularly powerful way for me in 1989.

A striking experience

I was deeply shocked on that day in 1989 when it was announced that SKB was going to merge with Beecham. I could not understand, at that time, why such a great and thriving business had come to the point where it had to give up its identity in order to survive. What were the senior executives of the company doing to get us into such a mess? There was a great sense of loss, anguish and failure. We all seemed to be doing our very best and yet it was just not good enough. This event had a significant impact on my life and on the relationships that I had built up in my organization over many years. It jolted my sense of what it was that made people in business successful.

I thought about how the situation had been managed in an attempt to figure out what it was that we had done wrong. None of this seemed to help. In many cases it seemed that what we had been doing complied with accepted recipes for success, yet we had failed to sustain our business in its own right. Even more frustrating was what seemed to be a complete disconnect between the feelings many of us were experiencing at the time and what I read, which seemed so cold and distant. Here I was involved in a real life drama of huge proportions and there seemed to be nowhere I could turn to in the management "body of knowledge" to help me make sense of what was happening at an ordinary day-to-day level.

How was it that highly paid and seemingly wise and experienced people, who I had respected greatly, had lost control of the situation? What were they doing up there? How could they let us all down so badly when we were doing everything we felt they needed us to do to ensure success? The teams I belonged to at the time were hitting new output records in manufacturing and our costs were coming down. How could it be that we had to merge with this other company that we all knew was second rate compared to our operation? I was in uncharted territory and feeling quite insecure as a result.

This experience raised, for me in a very powerful way, the question of control. In this book, I attempt to address the basic question of whether managers are in control of their business or not, one which has troubled me since the merger occurred. This is coupled to another question: is there any way to ensure that such events do not happen again, or do I have to accept that it is not possible to manage events to ensure success in the way I had thought?

Real life management: making it up as we go along

Prior to the merger everything had seemed so orderly and in control. We all thought we knew our places and what we had to do to be successful in them. Suddenly it was as if we had gone over a cliff and nothing really made sense any more. During the merger, it seemed that we were making things up as we went along. There was nowhere to refer to for a prescription, and nobody seemed to have had any experience of doing what we were doing on the scale we were doing it. This was both exciting and unsettling at the same time. This experience drove me to take an interest in conversations and articles that seemed to offer a different perspective on the nature of management. It eventually led me to the sciences of complexity, which seemed to have potential for helping me to make sense of a world that was ordered but in which no one was "in control." As I explored notions from the complexity sciences, I began to realize that on their own these new sciences would be no more successful in helping me make sense of my experience than those of my original scientific training as a chemist. They were not going to reveal any more to me than I had already found in the accepted classics of management. Potentially, I was going to be stuck in a rather unproductive and frustrating loop unless I could find another way.

Casting around for other ways of thinking, I began to explore the notion of dialogue. In fact, I found this so interesting that I joined a group of like-minded people who met informally in an attempt to make more sense of change at SmithKline Beecham (SB). It seemed that the most meaningful route to making sense of my question would be to explore experiences in dialogue with the material I was reading and with some of the people I was meeting in a doctoral group at the University of Hertfordshire. Since then, I have been attaching increasing importance to participation in reflective dialogue with people in my day-to-day work practice, with others in my research community and with the written word. I have come to see this activity as central to effective management. I have deliberately kept myself in the stories in this book because I have become increasingly convinced that it is not possible to separate the "reality" out there from myself "in here."

The key argument

In the stories of my experience in the following chapters, I hope to convey the paradoxical position in which managers find themselves, namely, that of being simultaneously "in control" and "not in control" of their business. I also hope to convey something of the emotion and anxiety of living with this paradox. I believe that when managers are able to live with this paradox, the resulting tension opens up the potential for new patterns of meaning, which carry the organization forward. Originally, I thought that the effective manager was one who was "in control" of predictable outcomes. This view dominated my thinking at the time of the merger. It seemed to me to be obvious that somebody must be "in control" of SKB. It was unthinkable that perhaps nobody was. I now believe that being "in control" is an illusion and that no one was in control of SKB in any simple sense. Having reached this insight, the danger is to move to the other extreme and conclude that there is no control at all. In this book, I seek to avoid that extreme as I attempt to explain the paradox of control, holding the tension between mainstream thinking – "manager in control" – and the other possibility – "manager not in control." I argue for a perspective that understands an organization in terms of complex responsive processes of relating, which enables me to avoid collapsing to either pole of the paradox.

For me, management has come to mean living with both sides of the control paradox at the same time. This means acting on the basis of an expectation of an outcome, knowing full well that it is unlikely to materialize, requiring me to be ready to handle the consequences whatever they may be. It involves developing effective ways of handling the anxiety of "not knowing."

It seems to me that we, as individuals, have a fundamental need to feel "in control" of situations in which we find ourselves. This need for control is connected to the experience of anxiety, in that the individual need for some sense of control is a way of dealing with the anxiety of not knowing. Since this anxiety is too powerful for most of us to meet on our own, we project our needs for control onto our organization in the hope that it will provide a sense of being "in control" and so defend us against anxiety. We generate the illusion of being in control through a variety of tactics such as talking to others to see if we can modify their behavior to suit us. We measure things in the hope that this tells us whether they are performing as we would wish. We design and attempt to impose our own patterns on the world in the hope that this makes it more predictable and we set targets or goals which we hope come to fruition. We try to emulate patterns of behavior that we believe to be connected to particular achievements in the hope that repeating these patterns will lead predictably to repeated success. When we go to work we try to remove emotions from the workplace, believing that if they are expressed they will open up a Pandora's box of not being in control. The fear is that this would lead people to become dysfunctional instead of working in an aligned fashion. We seem to need to believe that since an organization consists of many potentially diverse elements, there has to be some way of ensuring that all the parts work together for the good of the whole and to deliver for the business overall. Without the control exercised by those in positions of authority, we fear that the organization will not succeed since it will lack purpose and direction.

Mainstream thinking about management approaches the matter of uncertainty by trying to eliminate it through the creation of powerful hierarchies that are supported by the generation of huge amounts of information intended to reduce unknowns and to quantify risks of potential unknowns so that decisions can be made about them if they do arise. This tends to lead to detailed control, which stems from the belief that order and certainty can be imposed on inherently disorderly situations. Major, inexplicable changes in our organization are experienced as very powerful blows to our personal security. Increasingly, organizations fail to adequately serve the purpose of defending us against the anxiety provoked by uncertainty. Instead, as managers, we have to find the courage to carry on participating creatively in the construction of new meaning, in spite of not knowing. This requires an alternative explanation to mainstream thinking, which makes sense only in a world in which it is possible to be in control.

In my exploration of a possible alternative perspective, that of complex responsive processes of relating, I will be highlighting the following points:

- The paradoxical position in which managers find themselves. They are both "in control" and "not in control" at the same time.
- Thinking of an organization as complex responsive processes of relating in which patterns of meaning emerge. Conversations between those working together are the primary form of communicative interaction in organizations in which transient patterns of meaning emerge.
- The qualities of relationships, the influence of power, fantasies and searches for new meaning, all greatly influence conversational interactions. The actions managers take flow from the meaning they make of the circumstances in which they find themselves.

Outline of the book

Chapter two tells the story of my first experience of line management when I became responsible for the production of one of the company's products at a factory in Welwyn Garden City. Even at that level, where I thought that I could exercise control over product quality, I started to encounter the paradox of control. I found that in the living present of actual local production situations, there are always the "unknowns," no matter how well a procedure or process is defined in advance, that is, "known." In other words, this experience was paradoxically known – the designed procedure – and unknown – the variations around it – at the same time. There was, therefore, a requirement for those of us in the production department to live with the unknown, to make sense of the impact of unknown sources of variation and compensate so as to ensure that the production process as engineered actually worked. The effectiveness of the process depended crucially on operators who had learned how to cope with, or compensate for, some degree of uncertainty. In these circumstances, performance may have seemed very controlled, but actually emerged from the interactions between the operators, the manager, the materials and the processes involved.

In chapter three, I move to the other end of the management hierarchy and recount what I have been able to learn about the events leading up to the merger between SKB and Beecham. The story told in this chapter about management at the highest levels is similar in many ways to the story told in the previous chapter about management at the lowest hierarchical level. In my view, both reflect the paradox of control. The story of product development, marketing success and mergers, cannot be told simply in terms of intention in relation to known, predictable situations. An adequate account of what happened has to include the responses evoked and provoked by others and the uncertainty, indeed unknowability, of many aspects of the situations in which people were interacting. Mainstream literature presents explanations primarily in terms of intention and certainty, while largely ignoring their opposites. In practice, however, it is these simultaneously present opposites that managers must live with. It is the lack of congruence between the focus of attention of mainstream thinking about management and the lived experience of managing that calls for an alternative explanation. The SKB story told in this chapter seems to me to be an excellent example of the amplifying co-evolving processes that complexity scientists are seeking to understand. I draw on analogies with "fitness landscapes" to make sense of the evolution of SKB.

Chapter four takes up my personal experience of the post-merger situation at SB. I use two episodes to convey a sense of what it was like. The first is the formulation of three-year plans just after the merger, and the second describes how we went about rationalizing production. For most of us, the merger created a sense of losing control over our lives, a threat to vitally important aspects of the quality of our lives, as levels of uncertainty rose significantly. This resulted in rising anxiety and increased searching for ways to regain control over what seemed to be key aspects of our lives. My experience of the merger of SKB and Beecham indicates that much evolved in the interpersonal interactions that took place during the merger process as each of us struggled to make our own meanings in the circumstances in which we found ourselves. It is my belief that no amount of planning could have reduced this "messiness," which seemed to be a necessary and natural part of developing a new sense of purpose and place with my new colleagues. The disruption and reconfiguration of relationships and informal power patterns I experienced in the merger process seemed to be self-organizing in nature and dependent on how people formed their relationships under high levels of uncertainty. It was up to people in many different parts of the organization to respond in meaningful ways, and we did not immediately know what a meaningful response would be. Hence the many conversations that took place, in which we sought to create new meanings in local situations in the living present. The evolving identity of the integrating companies emerged in the interaction between all of these local situations.

The experiences described in chapters two, three and four led to my dissatisfaction with mainstream thinking and its avoidance of paradox. In chapter five, I summarize a perspective in which paradox is central. From this point of view, an organization is thought of as complex responsive processes of relating. These ideas emerged in the work of a group of doctoral students at the University of Hertfordshire, of which I was a member, and is set out in earlier volumes in this series (Stacey *et al.*, 2000; Stacey, 2001).

In chapter six, I take up another story, this time my experience of participating in a project to develop performance measures called Project Dashboard. By that time I was coming to think and act in a way that was more informed by the evolving perspective I have summarized in chapter five. The experience of Project Dashboard points to the central importance of the conversations in developing the meaning of what we were doing. In the course of talking about performance measures we were addressing many issues that were evolving in the emerging business situation and an important part of that situation was how power relations were shifting, what people were feeling about this, and how they were responding to those shifts. The theme of performance measures immediately triggered many other themes to do with performance in its wider sense. It was quickly linked to themes, also patterning many other conversations, to do with supply chains and logistics. What I describe is an ongoing process in which it is not possible to identify the beginning or the end. Instead there is a process in which meaning emerges in the known–unknown of the business context.

Chapter seven provides a short account of a budget meeting for a supply chain initiative called the Enterprise project. Being simultaneously "in control" and "not in control" is exemplified by the Enterprise budget meeting. Each person arriving at the meeting considers the others to be more or less competent. They vest in each other the notion that each is "in control" of their part of the project. Each has an implicit expectation that when another promises to deliver, they will. Those higher up in the hierarchy also implicitly assume that this team is in a position to control the project and its outcomes. The expectation is that projects tightly managed to deliver on time and to budget will improve the business. In one sense, then, managers are proceeding as if there is nothing paradoxical about control. However, the paradox of control is revealed by the pattern of conversation at the meeting. Instead of being a logical, crystal clear, straightforward management exercise, the meeting displays all of these characteristics and their opposites at the same time.

Chapter eight compares mainstream and complex responsive processes perspectives on the nature of management. For me the latter resonates more with my experience and therefore provides a more useful way of making sense of that experience. The central notion of mainstream thinking, that of the manager being "in control," is much more problematic than is usually assumed because managers are both "in control" and "not in control" at the same time. The key question then becomes how organizations operate effectively and maintain an orderly state of affairs if their managers are not simply "in control." From the perspective of complex responsive processes, it is transiently stable, self-organizing patterns of meaning that maintain a sense of order and therefore a sense of control as managers go about their daily activities. Intentional goal oriented acts emerge in the conversations of managers at a local level and those conversations function as patterning, meaning making processes. These communicative interactions constitute the way in which managers, individually and collectively, maintain their sense of self and their defenses against anxiety. An organization is self-organizing processes in which intention and meaning emerge and anxiety is lived with. These interconnected processes across an organization generate collective emergent outcomes that cannot be traced back to specific actions. Processes of change and performance achievement emerge in the self-organizing patterns of meaning in which each individual struggles in participation with others to maintain a sense of self in an uncertain world. The paradox of being "in control" and "not in control" at the same time pervades all hierarchical levels in the organization: the individual; individuals in conversation; the department level; the business unit level; the corporate level; and the industry level. The defining feature of management is not simply being "in control," but rather the courage to carry on participating creatively in spite of "not knowing."

2 Controlling quality?

- Getting the feel of it in practice: Contac 400
- Turning for guidance to the literature on quality control
- Local communicative interaction in the living present

In this chapter I reflect on my experience of first line management. When I took up my first management role it was my unquestioned expectation that I would be "in control" of the department I had been given responsibility for. I was to discover that being "in control" was far more problematic than I had imagined.

Getting the feel of it in practice: Contac 400

In the late 1980s, I moved from my role as an analytical chemist to manage a department manufacturing Smith Kline & French's (SK&F) Contac 400, the capsule filled with tiny time pills that are slowly released to stop your cold in its tracks! The manufacture of these capsules was a highly technical operation, supported by well-qualified engineers, process pharmacists and operators. The manufacturing process was defined in detail, and carefully validated and controlled to quality standards second to none. When I took up my position as manager of the department, I believed that it was my role to understand the processes, take responsibility for them, and control my department's outputs so that they were on budget, on time, and of the right quality. I believed that all I had to do was to ask the operators and they would tell me precisely how the pellets for the capsules were produced. However, I soon discovered that if I was to understand the process, I would have to join the team and work with the operators, under their guidance, as we manufactured the product together. I began to realize how much production performance on any particular day depended upon the detailed judgments that the operators were making about each step in the manufacturing process. The uncomfortable realization began to dawn on me that I was not actually in control of the department's performance in many significant ways, although I was certainly in charge of it and responsible for it. I learned that developing a mutually respectful relationship with the operators was more important than specifically controlling the production process. What led me to this realization?

Meeting the specifications for Contac capsules requires the mix of pellets to be kept consistent as the capsules are filled. However, the pellets had a tendency to separate as the capsules were filled. When I tried to find out why this happened, I was told that the process was the most secret one in the company and I began to realize that this really meant that no one fully understood it. Yet we were able to produce the product. I could not believe this! Surely we could specify the process in detail. After all we had been making the product for over thirty years. Convinced of this, I took a scientific approach to solving the separation problem. I worked on the production pans with the operators to get a feel for the product. The process involved spraying sugar solution onto sugar crystals and building up a pellet with coating powders including the drug substance. I was told that knowing when the pellets were wet enough to apply the powder, and yet not too wet, was the key to meeting specification. How did the operators know this? They watched and felt the beds of pellets and just knew when a batch was going to turn clumpy (too wet) or when powder would fly off up the extracts (too dry).

I conjectured that it was the relative size and densities of the different colored pellets in the mixture that was causing problems in the production of properly mixed sets of pellets to be filled into the capsules. My scientific approach to solving this problem was to analyze the process into a sequence of steps and ascertain the most likely causes of demixing. These causes related to pellet size and density, and to vibration during filling. I then focused on these aspects, intending to make the production process more robust.

We tried to control pellet size by monitoring the temperature and humidity of airflows through the coating pans in order to determine when coating powder should be added. It turned out that the pellet weights in the coating pans and initial crystal size range in the raw materials were somehow having an effect. We would have to go back to British Sugar to get them to change their sugar production process and standardize their output! They told us that they were delivering the natural spread of sugar crystal sizes and there was nothing they could do about it. So, we would have to sieve the sugar coming in to get the control we needed. We then set up measurement systems to control the automatic application of powders to standardize the production process. No matter how much we measured and attempted to control, we could not recreate the sensing/knowing of the operator in keeping the balance between powder lost up the air extract and powder that stuck to the pellets. Our yields (and therefore costs) were never as good as the operator achieved.

It then dawned on us that the very feature we were trying to remove actually played a critical role in determining the required characteristics of the product. We were trying to remove the variations in pellet size but this was vital in producing the variable release patterns in the stomach, the very feature that made the product a success. We did not know, and could not determine, the optimum size for each pellet because the release profile was the outcome of the interaction between all the pellets as they slowly dissolved together. There were so many interrelated factors influencing the product, process and operators that it became virtually impossible to separate and optimize any particular one in practice. We were unable to bring about consistent and sustainable control over this process and its outputs. Logically we could identify and implement some cause and effect relationships, but the product quality would then shift in a way we could not explain. It became clear why the process had not been more clearly specified before.

This rather chastening experience impressed on me the value of the kind of knowing that operators had developed over the years. Although we had built models of the production processes, which predicted some of the characteristics of the products, we could not make the practical jump from the model to the actual process. This experience left me somewhat unsettled and yet still believing that the "unsatisfactory" outcome was due to my not asking the right questions. However, despite the outcome, I somehow acquired a reputation for scientific thinking in this area and was sent to Japan as an expert to look at their production processes and provide support to them! Looking back on it now, this experience has all the features of the paradox of control and my response to it was typical of mainstream thinking about management.

Turning for guidance to the literature on quality control

As I now reflect on this experience, I see that I believed in an objectively knowable world very much independent of myself. I thought that I ought to be able to understand an objectively given process through building models of it and that this would then enable me to control the process. In this way, I thought I could ensure that my department produced predictable outputs. I would then be able to improve efficiency and manage costs more effectively. I hoped that others would perceive me to be a more effective manager than my predecessors, so bolstering my promotion prospects. My scientific background led me to believe that I ought to be able to identify the key variables and define the parameters I had to manipulate in order to gain control of the process. My approach at that time was very much in line with what I had been taught about process control logic and quality control through quality assurance (Ishikawa, 1985). This approach involved a study of variations in the quality of outputs from a production process, identification of the causes of the variations and the use of statistically based experiments (Box *et al.*, 1978) to ascertain appropriate ranges for the variables to be controlled. Steps could then be taken to keep the process within appropriate ranges and so under control. This logic underpins the Quality Control and the Total Quality Management movements (see Neave, 1990; Scholtes, 1992; Juran and Gryna, 1993; Soin, 1992) and they constitute a framework that still structures management thinking. I want to take a brief look at their development before reflecting on how they help or hinder my understanding of what I was involved in.

Deming (1982, 1986) pioneered Total Quality Management (TQM) in the early 1980s and Juran (1991) later developed his thinking. Deming exhorted organizations to remove fear and return self-esteem, dignity, and joy to the work of employees (Aguago, 1991). He thought of learning as an ongoing organization-wide activity in which all members were engaged (Anderson *et al.*, 1994). However, he linked these views to an emphasis on structured, formalized approaches to sharing knowledge across an organization so as to achieve the basic goal of reducing variability in order to gain control (Deming, 1993). Some hailed this as a new paradigm in management (Broedling, 1990), an alternative to simple management by control (Hunt, 1993; Price, 1989), indeed a new way of thinking about the management of an organization (Chorn, 1991). Some talked about new process-managed, customer-oriented organizations run by teams (Scholtes, 1992) and conducted more like ballets than hockey games (Slater, 1991). Some interpreted TQM in humanistic, systems terms (Brocka and Brocka, 1992) while others emphasized its technical (McMillen, 1991) and mechanistic aspects (Motsika and Shalliff, 1990).

However, many have been skeptical of the TQM movement (Choi and Behling, 1997) and a survey of the manufacturing and services sectors in the US suggested that only one-third of the 500 executives questioned actually believed that TQM enhanced competitiveness (Matthews and Katel, 1992). Another survey of 100 British firms found that only one-fifth believed that their TQM programs had a significant impact (Economist, 1992). Florida Power and Light, the company held up to be the leader in applying the TQM approach in the US, "slashed its quality department staff from 85 employees to 3 after group chairman James L. Broadbent found that many employees feared that the quality improvement process had become a tyrannical bureaucracy" (Choi and Behling, 1997: 37). Detractors pointed to the undue focus of TQM practitioners on control of processes rather than outcomes (Olian and Rynes, 1991), arguing that it shifted the focus too much from delivery to continuous improvement. Others argued that TQM had been oversold, inevitably leading to disappointment (Doyle, 1992).

Supporters of the TQM movement, however, ascribed any failure to managers who were saying that they were implementing TQM when in fact they were doing no such thing (Becker, 1993). Others suggested corrective actions to improve TQM, such as placing greater emphasis on assuring job security during the introduction of TQM (Doyle, 1992), developing more appropriate selection and training policies (Holpp, 1989; Bowen and Lawler, 1992; Schonberger, 1994), or taking more account of the complexity of the changes involved (Numeroff, 1992). Yet others focused on the seeming inability of managers to establish and generate a broad understanding of the organization's mission, goals and objectives (Pherson, 1994).

Spencer argues that: "some individuals may choose (consciously or not) to apply TQM mechanistically – particularly if they treat it as a set of principles, use the chain of command to audit and control static organizational activities, pay more attention to processes than customers, or place undue emphasis on organizational efficiency" (Spencer, 1994: 453). She suggests that this is a limited view of TQM as a functionalist doctrine that structures individual behavior to fit the demands of a larger system. She feels that this perspective does not accord with the intent of most quality experts and promoters and suggests an interpretive perspective, one that recognizes the social processes through which meaning is created (also see Barley et al., 1988).

When I ask myself what this vast literature is telling me about the situation I found myself in as the manager of the production department, faced with the important issue of quality, I hear a number of voices. The loudest voice is the one most consistent with my scientific background. It talks about the analysis I should do in order to design the procedures that will enable me to be in control of product quality. The goal this voice proclaims is that of reducing variation. Not quite so loud, but nevertheless insistent, is the voice reminding me of the operators and how I should think of them as members of a team engaged in an organization-wide learning process, providing them with proper training and motivation. An even softer voice suggests that operators and managers are together engaged in social, interpretive processes in which we are making meaning. It all leaves me with the distinct impression that I ought to be in control and that the goal of that control is to increase predictability and so reduce variation. I am supposed to know what to do and the possibility that I might have to live, somehow, with not knowing does not feature.

I want to draw attention to particular concepts that appear over and over again in the prescriptions for managing quality. They all have to do with being "in control":

- The position of the manager is that of an *individual who objectively observes* the production process.
- The manager *intentionally designs* these processes.
- The processes so designed are to be *predictable* so that the manager can deal with *certainty/the known*.
- The aim is to reduce variability so producing *conformity*.
- Conformity is sustained through *detecting/correcting deviation*.

The question to ask now is whether perspectives in the literature are useful in making sense of my experience of first line management.

Using the literature to make sense of experience

Applying the above TQM logic to the materials in the Contac production process described above was relatively easy. Armed with tests of particle size, as well as analytical purity and density, it was not difficult to determine many properties of the materials themselves, when studied in isolation from each other. The problems really began, however, when the materials were mixed. It then became extremely difficult to predict the outcomes of their interaction. The pellets had been produced for thirty years and when we looked at the records of equipment settings, material weights and temperatures, we found some guidance. There certainly were procedures for quality control and the track record for quality was good. However, records were quite fuzzy about what was actually supposed to happen in the production activity itself. Once the pans were loaded, the instructions simply said "apply coating powders until process complete." As we tried a variety of different approaches to understand what was going on in the production process, more and more resources were diverted into trying to define what was happening, to the point where it was not cost effective to search any further. In other words, it was economically better to live with the variability and occasional failure than to spend effort on trying to improve control. The more variables we discovered the more it became impossible to assess, let alone control, them all. The payback was just not there. In fact, then, we had to live with not knowing alongside knowing. Furthermore, not only was it too costly to remove the variability, as TQM so strongly advises, it would have been counterproductive to do so. What I learned from my attempts to reduce variability in this particular production process was that the final product required a degree of variation in the process if the product was to serve its purpose adequately.

The conclusion I draw is that technically well-defined processes, such as pellet and capsule manufacture, assumed to be solid and certain in the literature, are really highly interactive technical and human processes. It is the interaction of the operators, as they jointly bring together their skills, the equipment and the materials, to form a process that works regularly enough to be economically viable. This process was actually highly successful in producing a product within required limits. For me, at that time, believing that everything ought to be defined in advance and that I ought to be "in control," in line with what I had been taught, the pellet process felt like some kind of failure.

Note how the description of my actual experience brings in concepts additional to those emphasized by the literature on quality control, indeed ones that are direct contradictions in that they are all about "not being in control":

- The position of the manager is that of *participant in group interactions* in the production process.
- The manager responds *in ways evoked or even provoked* by features of the process and the human interactions it involves.
- The processes are sometimes *unpredictable* so that the manager must deal with *uncertainty/the unknown*.

- The aim is not simply reducing variability because *deviations* are also valuable.
- It follows that *diversity* may be as important as conformity.

While the literature on quality management relies entirely on concepts to do with being "in control" and prescribes the removal of the features of "not being in control," my experience suggests that the latter features are not only irremovable but also valuable. In other words, I am arguing that my experience cannot be understood purely in terms of "being in control" because that experience was also one of "not being in control" in important ways. If I stay with mainstream views of always needing to be "in control," I can only conclude that I failed and this simply does not feel right. It would also not feel right to argue that I was "not in control" at all. Perhaps I can make more sense of my experience if I come to understand management as a paradox of "being in control" and "not being in control" at the same time.

What I want to begin to point to now, is a perspective that I think enables me to understand the sense in which the process I have been describing was indeed a success. It is a perspective that enables me to see that an exclusive way of thinking to do with being "in control" is not a very helpful way of understanding the management role.

Local communicative interaction in the living present

As an analytical chemist and experienced bench analyst, I understood the production process from a procedural, analytical and production formulation viewpoint. This was scientific, technical knowledge in the form of propositions, and I initially privileged this as the only valid knowledge. However, the operators talked about the production process as more of an art than a science and I soon discovered that my scientific kind of knowledge was not enough. I had to work with the production operators, to learn with them about the production process. In other words, I had to engage in situated learning in which one "acquires the skill to perform by actually engaging in the process under the conditions of legitimate peripheral participation – which denotes the engagement of a learner who participates in the actual practice of an expert, but only to a limited degree and with limited responsibility for the ultimate product as a whole" (Hanks, 1994: 14). This is a view of learning as "increasing participation in communities of practice . . . [as] . . . the whole person acting in the world" (Lave and Wenger, 1994: 49). From this perspective, learning is an evolving process of participation, that is, of continuously renewed relations between people, their actions and the world. Such a theory emphasizes interdependency of actor, the world, activity, meaning, cognition, learning and knowing. Lave and Wenger describe learning as the "historical production, transformation, and change of persons" (51). A fundamental basis of their theory is that participation is always based on situated negotiation and renegotiation of meaning in the world. In many ways, this is a good description of what was going on as I worked with the operators on the processing problem we had. However, Lave and Wenger have a rather different notion of participation to mine. They understand people moving from non-participation to full participation in a bounded community of practice. My experience was that of a less structured evolution, a more ordinary process of talking together about the issues and trying to make sense of what was happening, as we sought to exercise more control over the process.

Looking back, I think I stumbled into developing more helpful relationships when I sometimes put aside my hierarchical role to work with some of the operators on the coating pans because I was so keen to understand what was happening. I did not realize it then, but in doing this I was behaving very differently from previous managers of the department. They had behaved in a detached manner and spent little time with the operators. I broke down some of the formal, hierarchical barriers by behaving very differently. At first, I was treated with suspicion, but then, as we got to know each other, more respect developed. I knew I had to rely on them and in return they could rely on me. This did not mean abdicating my authority as a manager. There were unofficial rules that kept everyone in line. Those who did not pull their weight, or who abused the rules, expected to be pulled back in line. I learned that it was part of my role to be the guardian of the line that we were together constructing, articulating that line and disciplining those who crossed it.

I realize now, on reflection, that what I thought was very solid – manager of department, in charge, in control – was not really the situation. I had to give up the solidness of my understanding of the role in order to be effective at it. Rather than keeping my distance, I had tried to connect more with people. Rather than using formally defined rules to keep discipline, I became part of a process of negotiation in a community in which I was given permission to do certain things that we all thought were for our mutual good. I had to rely on the capabilities of the operators and their motivations for success, not the well-defined and controlled processes that I originally thought were key. Together we lived with the uncertainty of the processes by building cushions where we could to enable us to cope, if and when things went wrong. We adjusted our behavior and production schedules, plus our stocks and declared targets, to allow us to create the image of being "in control" and yet behind the scenes, as it were, we were compensating for what we could not know, for what we could not control. For those outside, we projected an air of confidence that we knew how to deliver. Internally, our motto was under-promise and over-deliver, so that we had enough leeway to handle things when they went wrong and yet not be criticized or devalued because we were not running things properly.

The reason why it turned out to be inappropriate to think about my management role as something solid had very much to do with the nature of the knowledge required for the seemingly solid production process, which also turned out on close inspection to be fuzzy. The operators knew more about the production process than could possibly be recorded in process instructions and procedures (Brown and Duguid, 1991). It is not possible to describe the feeling of appropriate grittiness in powder, for example. You can only know this from experience. The same goes for the wetness of the pellet beds used in the process. You have to feel them to get to know them, to know when they are too wet or too dry. Yield consistency (and therefore department efficiency and product cost) is dependent upon this experience.

A previous volume (Stacey, 2001) in the series of which this book is a part, presents a perspective that is well illustrated, I believe, by what I have been talking about in this chapter. From that perspective, organization is understood as processes of communicative interaction in which people take joint action. We could only accomplish our joint task of producing product to required cost, time and quality through the action of communicating with each other in the living present in the local situation in which we found ourselves. The joint action of producing Contac pellets obviously required the use of tools: the pans, the drying equipment, the technology of production and so on. Less obviously, perhaps, are the tools required for the kind of communicative interaction upon which the more obvious action of production depends. In this case, the tools we used in communicatively interacting with each other were the rules and procedures set out for the production process and the required quality. Other, even less obvious tools took the form of informal rules about appropriate and inappropriate behavior. For me, the TQM literature tends to focus on the tools and loses sight of the processes of communicative interaction in which the tools are used. The point about communicative interaction in the living present is that it is to a significant extent spontaneous and so cannot proceed according to pre-established rules. Communicative interaction is the action one person takes in relation to another and the response of that other in a locally situated, continuous process of gesture and response as described in the earlier volume to which I have already referred (Stacey, 2001). It is in this process of communication that people cope in the living present with the inevitable variations of daily life.

The known–unknown and emergence

In the living present of actual local production situations, there are always the "unknowns," no matter how well a procedure or process is defined in advance, that is "known." In other words, this experience is paradoxically known – the designed procedure – and unknown – the variations around it – at the same time. There is, therefore, always the requirement for participants to live with the unknown, to somehow make sense of the impact of unknown sources of variation and compensate so as to ensure that the production process as engineered actually works. The effectiveness of the process depends crucially on operators who have learned how to cope with, or compensate for, some degree of uncertainty. In these circumstances, performance may seem very controlled, but will actually emerge from the interactions between the operators, the manager, the materials and the processes involved. The under-promise and over-deliver pattern described above enabled all to be seen to be successful while coping with the uncertainty inherent in both the materials and processes and also the relationships, which could fluctuate depending upon how people were feeling. In a sense the performance of the department evolved as all of these variables interacted.

I am arguing, therefore, that mainstream thinking, with its focus on "being in control" to the exclusion of features to do with "not being in control," is an inadequate way of making sense of the lived experience of first line management. A move to a way of thinking that places living with paradox at the center might be a more useful way of making sense of such an experience. I am suggesting that the manager is "in control" and "not in control" at the same time. By this I mean that the experience of managing is characterized by the simultaneous presence of the aspects summarized in Figure 2.1.

"in control"	"not in control"
Management action is:	*Management action is:*
Intended/selected/designed	Evoked/provoked response
Taken in relation to the:	*Taken in relation to the:*
Known	Unknown
Predictable/certain	Unpredictable/uncertain
Stable	Unstable
Regular	Irregular
Involving:	*Involving:*
Detecting/correcting deviation	Amplifying deviation
Producing:	*Producing:*
Conformity/consensus	Diversity/conflict

Figure 2.1 *The paradox of control in first line management*

Conclusion

The universal expectation seems to be that managers are "in control": operators expect the manager of the department to be in control; the department manager expects to be in control; the manager's boss expects him or her to be in control; she or he expects the boss to be in control; and so on up to the CEO.

However, my experience of control as manager at the departmental level leads me to see just how tenuous this notion of control is in practice. The role of manager as controller, in the sense of holder of knowledge, is limited by the access to the conversation around the production processes. The operator community had a common pattern of knowing around the basic manufacturing processes that was communicated in a language from which the manager could be excluded and would not even know existed. Pre-existing patterns of behavior had effectively locked out managers from gaining knowledge of, and from coming to know, these processes.

The inability of the technical assessment of the production process to bring about improved control through the identification and control of the key variables meant that the tasks carried out in the department were uncontrollable in any simple sense. The product effectively "emerged" from the variable combination of operator, material, equipment and environment settings or inputs. This made the meeting of commitments made by the department difficult.

The manager of the department was expected to make commitments to deliveries from an unstable production process. The expectation was that he, as the manager, would control the delivery of product to time, quality and cost. On an annual basis the department manager was expected to commit to an annual running cost for the department against uncertain volume projections. Performance seemed to emerge more from the interaction of events than by design. Over-production of product helped to maintain the sense of the department being "in control" and perpetuated the perception of reliability so important in achieving success as a manager.

The role of the manager in the department, while formally written down in a job description and appearing on an organization chart, was only loosely related to the formal definition. It seemed that I only became effective as a manager when I was able to distance myself somewhat from the role of "formal manager" and talk to the operators so that we could together make sense of what was happening. What then emerged in conversation, and patterns of behavior based on the sense made, became "the manager." Control in the sense of coordinated patterns of behavior and meaning then emerged in the relationships. Ultimately this seemed to be important for the achievement of our goals.

One might argue, however, that an understanding of quality management as a rational process of control works well enough and that emergent aspects are rather peripheral. But this argument faces much greater difficulties if one steps back, or rather steps higher up the management hierarchy, and asks how products, such as Contac 400, come about in the first place. This is the subject of chapter three.

3 The emergence of new products: the story of SmithKline Beckman and its merger with Beecham

- Passing judgment on SKB management
- New product development is supposed to be planned
- In fact new products and strategic directions emerge: drawing analogies from the complexity sciences

This chapter explores the question of control in relation to new product development and strategic direction. In early 1989, I was working in production management at one of SmithKline Beckman's (SKB) factories in the UK. My perspective on product development and strategic direction, therefore, was from a position well down the hierarchy, where the sense I was able to make of what was happening in the corporation as a whole depended upon the public communications issued by top executives and the reports and comments of analysts and journalists, as well as the usual informal stories and rumors. From this perspective, I want to explore the notion that the CEO and his leadership team are in control of the business, taking account of the following factors:

- The emergent nature of research and the implications of this emergence for R&D based pharmaceutical businesses.
- The co-evolving nature of a company and its environment as experienced in the attempts to keep SKB on course as an independent business.

Passing judgment on SKB management

In February 1989, Henry Wendt, the Chairman of SKB, met with highly critical analysts in Manhattan. The company's shares were worth no more than they had been in 1981 and Wall Street was looking for action. The journalist, Robert Teltman wrote:

> Wendt, silver haired, square jawed and immaculate as ever, was trying to convince yet another Wall Street audience that he had a workout plan for SmithKline Beckman. That he would unlock the value of its non-drug business and let investors share in the wealth with some form of tax free stock distribution. That they should look upon his proposed restructuring as a crucible of corporate revival.
>
> (Teltman, 1989: 31)

This article was very negative about SKB's future and so the shares fell to yet further lows. The company's history was described as "the sad tale of a lost opportunity and management incompetence. A company facing a slow liquidation or take-over when it should be reveling in the riches that were expected to come from its industry's biggest success" (Teltman, 1989: 31). What were the "biggest success" and the "lost opportunity and management incompetence"? The answer to this question lies in the company's history.

Smith, Kline and French (SK&F) was founded in 1830 in Philadelphia and by 1955 it was a company which had major brands in amphetamines and a tranquillizer called Thorazine. During the early 1960s, the company launched Contac, the product discussed in the last chapter. This enabled the company to expand its business into Japan where Henry Wendt spent time from 1966 to 1968 developing the business prior to becoming chairman. In 1968 Henry Wendt returned to the US having successfully established the business in Japan. In 1970, he visited the company's subsidiary in London and returned to the US with the news of that subsidiary's discovery of a compound that shut off the flow of stomach acid. This discovery, which led to the creation of Tagamet, promised to revolutionize ulcer treatment, and it is this that the journalist referred to as the "biggest success."

Tagamet: the success story

The story of Tagamet has been described as "a landmark example – the first time the intentional use of rational drug designs from first principles was applied in science" (Hall, 1997: 25). Indeed, the Royal Society of

Chemistry and the American Chemical Society designated it as the first international Historic Chemical Landmark.

However, was Tagamet really the result of rational design from first principles, simply a triumph for the scientific method? I think the answer to this question is not all that simple. Consider some key events in the history of the development of this compound.

SK&F had already developed some knowledge in the area of ulcer treatment before the official start of work on what was to become Tagamet. SK&F's scientists had identified that histamine triggered the release of stomach acid when it is bound to receptors in the stomach lining. James Black (later a Nobel prize-winner) moved from ICI in 1964 to head a small SK&F research unit in the UK, where he started a research program to find histamine antagonists that would selectively inhibit acid secretion. Chemists (Graham Durant, Robin Ganellin and John Emmett) began work on synthesizing modified histamine molecules in order to assess their pharmacological effect. The team then stumbled on a molecular variant, which was in fact an agonist, that is, it increased the amount of acid secreted. However, it did so without having effects that other histamines had. This unexpected occurrence was the basis on which the team postulated a clear target for the drug research. Tagamet, therefore, was not the straightforward development of a scientific hypothesis well formulated in advance.

After the discovery of the agonist, Black thought that the team of chemists would have no problem finding and synthesizing potential histamine antagonists but it turned out to be more difficult than anticipated because nothing was known about the structure of the receptor in the stomach lining; only the basic structure of the histamine molecule was known. Using "plain old intuition the chemists set about coming up with structures that were similar to the histamine but that would be inactive at the receptor" (Hall, 1997: 27). So, although the development of this drug was hailed as a triumph for the rational, logical approach, it is clear that intuition also played an important role. The chemists struggled with the uncertainty of not knowing what the biologically significant behavior of histamine was, and by 1968 they had synthesized more than 200 compounds without success. The next step depended upon an insightful brainwave from one of the pharmacologists in the research team, Mike Parsons, who suggested some adjustments that finally produced a guanidine analogue of histamine (a compound that had previously been tested and discarded).

By 1972, the research team had produced a molecule called burimamide, which was an active antagonist. They took this further with the development of metiamide in 1973 and this was the compound they began using in clinical trials. Results from these trials showed a spectacular clear-up rate with ulcers gone within three weeks. The claim was that metiamide "was the culmination of a rigorous scientific investigation, in which chemists probed the subtle relationships between the electronic structure and shape of the candidate molecules under biological conditions" (Hall, 1997: 27). However, metiamide was not the final compound. There was one more twist. Metiamide contained a thiourea group as a side chain and this turned out to have a toxicity problem that caused a blood disorder, agranulocytosis. Fortunately, the team had taken the precaution of developing cimetidine alongside metiamide. Cimetidine, it turned out, did not have the toxicity of metiamide and became the treatment that the company took forward.

While this work proceeded, the company as a whole had to deal with the introduction of tighter regulation of drug development and the rapidly escalating costs of R&D. Struggling to maintain cash generation to fund ongoing research, the company was attempting to cut back payroll costs against a background of Thorazine going off patent in the US. With limited budgets, the future of Black's research was not assured, especially since it was being carried out in the UK, far from the controlling eyes of the business owners in the US. However, Black and his team managed to convince their backers that the science was valid and would pay off. Black's approach sounded convincing: determine the biochemistry involved in the disease state and then search for chemically derived interventions. Nevertheless, at the time of Henry Wendt's visit in 1970, Black's project was under threat of discontinuation. There was apparently an ultimatum that the project would be discontinued if it did not produce a viable compound by the end of 1971. Note here how the development of the new project was affected by what was going on in other aspects of the business and how its continuation depended on the political and negotiating skills of those who believed in it. There was no "scientific" guarantee that it would succeed.

However, the project did survive and the skills of those working on it, based on hard science, intuition, "insurance policies" and politics, produced a spectacular result in Tagamet. Commercially, the company was unprepared for what hit it. The product was launched in the UK at the Welwyn Garden City factory. The press response to this treatment created significant public awareness, which put pressure on doctors to prescribe the product. However, at the time of the product launch in 1976, the Welwyn Garden City factory could produce only a small volume of tablets and what was projected as six months' stock was sold in a week. Production facilities were rapidly expanded and Tagamet fuelled SK&F's sales growth from £330 million in 1976, to £1 billion in 1980, and £2.5 billion by 1989.

This brief account reveals much about the process of new product development. The process can be described in terms of intention and design but also in terms of responses evoked and provoked by other people and events. In some ways the development path was predictable and it certainly involved making predictions. But in other ways it was unpredictable. There were aspects of both the known and the unknown. It was a process of detecting and correcting deviations from the expected but also processes of amplifying unexpected developments. In other words, the development of Tagamet displayed the hallmarks of the paradox of control in an even more obvious way than the control of product quality described in the last chapter.

Tagamet, then, was "the biggest success" to which Teltman was referring. What then was the "lost opportunity and management incompetence"?

Lost opportunity and management incompetence

By the early 1980s the R&D pipeline at SK&F was not yielding a significant enough contribution to the business and so diversification was adopted as the way forward. Almost as a sideline, the company began acquiring a collection of small clinical laboratories in the 1970s. This continued through the 1980s along with the acquisition of the Allergan eye-care business and the purchase of Beckman instruments for $1 billion, both in 1982. Analysts found the acquisitions difficult to match to a coherent strategy in the sense that SK&F had been sending out conflicting messages of diversification on one hand, and concentration on its R&D activities on the other. The Beckman purchase did not turn out well and between 1982 and 1984 the company, now SmithKline Beckman (SKB), was unable to generate growth. Indeed, by 1984 there was a 40 percent drop in Beckman's operating profits due to the contracting hospital market in the US.

Furthermore, SKB was considered myopic by some observers, since it appeared not to respond effectively to potential competitors for Tagamet.

In 1982, Glaxo launched Zantac, which was claimed to have a cleaner side-effect profile than Tagamet. Glaxo was a relatively unknown company in 1982 and was "underestimated by SmithKline in a big way" according to Jonathan Gelles, an analyst at Wertheim Schroder (SG Warburg, 1988: 2). During the period of most rapid market growth, SmithKline had increased prices at regular intervals. The arrival of a hungry competitor in the market-place exposed this approach. Glaxo attacked on two fronts: in marketing and in regulatory affairs. SmithKline was also slow at expanding the potential use of Tagamet by filing for usage extensions, while Glaxo increased the market by achieving approved claims for Zantac in conditions like heartburn, for example. In 1988 Tagamet sales crashed because the pharmaceutical distributors had stocked up in 1987 in anticipation of SmithKline raising Tagamet prices to compensate for the loss of other drug sales. From mid-1988 onwards the trade de-stocked so that SmithKline effectively lost sales volume at that time. The Wall Street analyst, Teltman, commented: "Henry Wendt and Robert Dee briefly got lucky, but they failed to capitalize on it. For SmithKline Beckman it is back to the minor league" (Teltman, 1989: 31). This assessment was reinforced by the SG Warburg securities recommendation for SmithKline Beckman in August 1988:

> SmithKline now sells at substantial discounts to all our traditional valuation measures of price-to-sales, price-to-stated net income, price-to-cash flow and price-to-book value and to our non-traditional measures of market share position and research resources. On our estimated break-up value, SmithKline barely sells at the low end of our range. Thus SmithKline has become an attractive take-over candidate. In other words should the SmithKline management fail to do a thorough restructuring job, we believe somebody else will do it for them. From a shareholder's perspective this is the most attractive alternative. Should SmithKline be taken over then the share price could reach $73 a gain of 55%!
>
> (1988: 1)

These, then, were the developments judged by journalists to be the "lost opportunity and management incompetence." The judgment implies that managers could have known what the outcome of an acquisition would be and that they could have predicted the behavior of a competitor. In other words, the judgment implies that it was possible for managers to be "in control." But is this judgment of incompetence as simplistic as the attribution of the "success" of the Tagamet discovery purely to the scientific method? I think the answer to this question is yes, and my reasons for this answer have much to do with the inherently uncertain nature of new product development and the impossibility of controlling competitor responses. Consider what happened to the intentions announced for new products at the end of 1988.

Prospects for the future

In December 1988, the company management magazine *Communiqué* (vol. 9, no. 9) carried an article in which the SKB management team articulated their views on the future. Short-term opportunities were described at that time as follows (a comment on what subsequently happened is given in brackets):

- Neuromet will be marketed in several countries across Europe and possibly in the US. (This product was never commercialized.)
- Broader marketing rights will be developed for Calcitonin in Europe, Canada and Australia. (This was never sold outside Italy.)
- Ridaura offers potential for treatment of bronchial asthma patients. (Ridaura contained gold and had a toxicity profile associated with the metal, which prevented its extension. Costs were also prohibitive. The product was disposed of in various licensing deals over time.)
- Algitec, a combination of cimetidine and alginic acid, will be launched in the UK in January and a dossier will be submitted in other European countries. (The product was launched in the UK but never achieved its target sales. Shifts in reimbursement policy by the UK Government effectively blacklisted the product only months after its launch. The cost to the patient, plus technical problems with the alginic acid gelling at low temperatures, undermined the product and confined it to a niche status. Only two other markets attempted to do anything with the product.)
- Engerix B is scheduled for introduction in the US and France in the first quarter of 1989. Sales projections are conservative but, according to Fred Kyle, Executive Vice President Operations, "the product is significant from a strategic standpoint because it puts us in the US vaccine business – it has real implications for the future." (This was an understatement as it turned out. In 1992 its sales grew by 154 percent. It had "an extraordinary year." The early launch phase was massively influenced by Merck's production and supply problems with its blood-derived product. This generated the opportunity for Engerix to monopolize the hepatitis B market for almost a year. By 1998 the sales

of the vaccines business, of which Engerix was a major part, hit £1 billion per annum.)

- "The vaccines business will grow significantly over the next five years through aggressive marketing and the addition of new products. Vaccines for pertussis and hepatitis A are now in human clinical trials and should come to the US and Europe market within 3 years. Within four years we can probably have a hepatitis A–B combination on the market," according to Bill Packer, Vice President Biologicals. (The pertussis and hepatitis A aspirations were achieved. Havrix, the hepatitis A vaccine also outstripped all expectations, making it the second largest product in the vaccine portfolio by value. The A–B combination was made available to market in 1997.)

- "New product forms and indications assure continued growth for Tagamet. We are moving as rapidly as possible towards non-ulcer uses as well. There are plans to submit three registration files for Cimetidine to the FDA in the near future; one for dyspepsia; one for gastrointestinal reflux disease; and one for healing erosions associated with NSAIDs." (This was too late. Glaxo had already established these claims and were actively using them to both expand the market for the histamine antagonists and erode Tagamet's share of the market.)

- "Progress continues to be made towards OTC Cimetidine, which Goddard (Vice President Worldwide Strategic Marketing) calls the ultimate downstreaming of Tagamet." (This hit the market in 1995 and proved too late. Sadly, it made over-the-counter status only months ahead of its rivals whereas back in 1976 SK&F was at least six years ahead of the nearest potential competitor.)

- "Major therapeutic investment is in the cardiovascular area. The New Drug Application (NDA) for intravenous 'Corlopam' for hypertension was filed in early December. The NDA for the oral form of the drug – for congestive heart failure – will be filed next year." (This compound did not make it past the NDA phase of development.)

- "Kredex for hypertension has been submitted for registration in nearly a dozen European countries. An international launch is planned for early 1990." (This product was in-licensed from Boehringer. It was only launched in Belgium and the Nordic markets for hypertension in early 1992. Kredex disappeared from sight strategically as an opportunity and therefore never really contributed. Then, in 1995 the product re-emerged as a treatment for congestive heart failure. A study in the US indicated it was so effective that it was saving lives.)

In a final section of the article, Fred Kyle states: "We've gone through uncertainty and changes, we've had to make difficult decisions. I don't think anybody wants to go through that unless they think it is reasonable and good for the business, good for the majority of our people, and that it will lead to this company being better placed in the future." President John Chappel adds: "With the people we now have on board, we can proceed to do what must be done. Not only can we do it, but we can do it much faster than many people give us credit for."

Notice in the above list of drug developments how unexpected most of the eventual outcomes were and how much they depended upon what competitors, governments and regulatory authorities did, not to mention unexpected properties of the compounds themselves. Outcomes depended not just on what managers at SKB did but on what people in other organizations were doing too. Outcomes may have been predictable to some extent but in very important ways they were unpredictable. Does it make sense to applaud top managers when an unexpected success emerges and condemn them as incompetent when unexpected difficulties emerge? It does from a way of thinking that ascribes success and failure to rational autonomous choices and conveniently downplays the enormous uncertainties of new product development. It does not from an alternative way of thinking, which I will come to later in this chapter, that places uncertainty at the center and understands the evolution of a company in terms of emergence.

The merger

On April 2, 1989, not three months after the publication of the strategic review discussed above, SKB and Beecham jointly announced that they were engaged in discussions concerning a possible merger of the two companies.

There are public records of the merger discussions in early 1989 between Henry Wendt, CEO at SKB, and Bob Bauman, CEO at Beecham, particularly *From Promise to Performance* (Bauman et al., 1997). The two chief executives met in a hotel room and talked about whether the new company should be a purely pharmaceutical one, or whether it should be an integrated healthcare company. Apparently they felt that the pharmaceutical industry was a "strong, stable industry, affected very rarely (if ever) by external events and thus had virtually no business cycles" (Bauman et al., 1997: 67). However, they also considered the precarious nature of companies within the industry, identifying dramatic cycles "driven by their propensity to pursue blockbusters. The lines on the sales charts would all be upward during patent protection, but the downturn would be precipitous once the patent was lost" (Bauman *et al.*, 1997: 67). Indeed, SKB entered the merger discussions for those very reasons. Bauman reports: "An integrated healthcare company promised greater stability, more consistent earnings flow, and less risk since more of the factors were in company control" (67). This integrated healthcare option, therefore, seemed safer to the two men and offered them more potential for controlling the flow of earnings. However, the combined companies would still have to deal with Tagamet coming off patent in the US in 1994.

As they talked, both men knew their futures hung in the balance. Bauman's star had been gradually rising as Beecham continued to deliver against each of its stated financial objectives. However, he could not see growth coming fast enough at Beecham to maintain this, thus threatening his aspiration to be seen as a successful CEO. Wendt was already out of favor in Wall Street because it looked as if SKB had been swinging from one position to another strategically, giving analysts the impression that senior managers were not in control of the business. They knew, therefore, that Bob would have to be chief executive, leaving Henry in the role of chairman, although they agreed that both would report directly to the board (Bauman *et al.*, 1997: 68). This alliance, struck on the basis of their own personal needs, created the best opportunity for them to sell the merger to the financial markets. The alternative could have been hostile bids for each partner company by others, resulting in both leaders being deposed. Bauman reports that this was "the most personally awkward and difficult of the questions to be resolved" (Bauman *et al.*, 1997: 68). After addressing this question, it was "time to address the business and financial issues" (68). In defining their own positions and agreeing them with each other, both men had taken steps to try to control their immediate futures. Secure in this knowledge, and having established sufficient trust between them, they were able to move forward. The basis of the initial merger work had much more to do with their relationship than it did with financial and business issues, which they tackled second! In announcing the merger, however, the reasons they gave for their respective roles were couched entirely in rational financial and business terms.

Bauman and Wendt then set about developing a merger process designed to control behavior in the organization, to control decision-making processes and remove emotion from them.

> The need for discipline and control versus a lot of activity during this
> time was heavily emphasized . . . Not every member of the MMC
> (Merger Management Committee) agreed with the tight discipline and
> control of the work plans. Some found the centralized process highly
> objectionable, especially where tradition had been to set targets for a
> unit but leave it to unit members to determine how they would
> generate the results.
>
> (Bauman *et al.*, 1997: 68)

They emphasized that the establishment of common ways of working was
essential to success since people had to come together from two very
different companies. They also said that discipline was needed to ensure
that integration teams used facts and data to support their
recommendations. Bauman wrote:

> just as important, they needed to get the emotion out of decisions . . .
> requiring team members to focus on gathering data . . . would force them
> to be more analytical in developing their recommendations. It meant
> looking to the future rather than the past. It kept personalities out of the
> process and focused them on achieving the goal of going for the best.
>
> (108)

Bauman was apparently at his most controlling at this point. He had
established his credibility with the financial markets by delivering
consistent results in line with managed expectations. As he reviewed the
first set of SB budget numbers he could see that the 15 percent growth
target in earnings per share would not be achieved. He would not accept
this. "SB's credibility as a new company and his credibility as its chief
executive were both at stake. Without tight controls, he felt SB would
never get the numbers it needed to satisfy the financial markets"
(Bauman *et al.*, 1997: 115).

It seems that the new CEO was much concerned with influencing the
analysts so that he could retain his position. It is striking how the top men
were trying to orchestrate an avoidance of actions driven by emotion and
personal career interests in the rest of the organization, when such factors
were clearly driving them.

New product development is supposed to be planned

How was I, years after the by then mythical development of Tagamet, and
geographically and hierarchically distant from the activity around share

prices and merger talks in early 1989, to make sense of what was going on? How was I to think about what I was reading and hearing in relation to my job at the time? Well, one source I could turn to was the literature on product development, mergers and planning in organizations. At the time I was studying part-time for an MBA, which exposed me to much of this literature. So, what does it have to say?

The evolution of the pharmaceutical industry depends upon research and development. Innovation is thus fundamental to the success of any organization in the industry. José Fonseca's forthcoming book *Complexity and Innovation in Organizations* points to three major positions taken by writers in the literature on innovation in general.

First, there is the managerial position, which regards innovation as a purposeful, adaptive procedure for attaining a future fit. This is based on the assumption that the innovative process is a form of rational, intentional and sequential logic. This school of thinking (e.g. Zirger and Maidique, 1990; Gupta and Wilemon, 1990; Crawford, 1991) supports its arguments with empirical evidence of best practice approaches to innovation management. Drucker (1986) also advocates a systematic approach to innovation as a key part of entrepreneurial behavior: "Systematic innovation therefore consists in the purposeful and organized search for changes, and in the systematic analysis of the opportunities such changes might offer for economic or social innovation" (49).

The second position has a technological orientation and assumes that knowledge is a crucial component of competition. The focus in this area tends to be typified by Wheelwright and Clark (1992) who use the concept of development funnels to focus management on the process of reducing the development time from recognition of the innovation to delivery to the market place. This thinking is an extension of the Hewlett Packard development project return map (House and Price, 1991), adopted by SB, for example, when it mounted a speed to market project with the aim of 2,000 days by the year 2000.

The third position sees innovation as social and political processes. For example, Kanter (1984, 1988) argues that uncertainty makes timing and costs so difficult to project that planning cannot be the main approach to managing the innovation process. She argues that leaders should develop the right environment to foster interactions in which tacit knowledge can be developed. Van de Ven (1988) suggests that there are four main problems that need to be resolved for successful innovation. The first is managing attention, by which he means the process in which some individual perceives some incongruence in the environment that might constitute an opportunity. Second, the finder of such an opportunity needs to build a critical mass of support and this requires the use of political processes. Third, many different kinds of resource must be combined to reconcile local and global needs. Finally, institutional leadership must build a shared culture and vision supportive of the first three activities. Frost and Egri (1991) highlight political processes and the ambiguity which surrounds the research process: "innovation at its core is about ambiguity and is replete with disputes caused by differences in perspectives among those touched by an innovation and the change it engenders. We believe that innovation often becomes a very political process" (231).

Relating specifically to pharmaceutical research and development, theorists have tended to focus mainly on the sequential, deliberate and rational processes. They have been searching for decades for improvements in R&D efficiency. Reekie (1975) made an intensive study of pharmaceutical firms and concluded that the size of the R&D effort is an important indicator of innovative output. Schwartzmann (1976) suggested that over the long term a large-scale approach might not be as profitable as multiple smaller efforts. Carter and Williams (1957), Myers and Marquis (1969), Utterback (1975) and Rothwell (1992) have all carried out comprehensive studies of the systematic general management of R&D in the industry. Decade after decade, they all come up with the same set of factors, or prescriptions to do with: installing good communication systems; implementing careful planning and project control procedures; implementing effective quality control systems; appointing effective product champions and technological gatekeepers; and high quality, dynamic managers with open minds and the ability to attract and retain talented researchers.

By the 1980s, risk management was introduced as another important factor. Grabowski and Vernon (1984) and Drews (1989) made explicit attempts to model R&D risk in pharmaceutical research. Merck & Co built this approach directly into their financial analysis models for research (Nichols, 1994) including Monte Carlo simulation techniques to aid management decision making. Zeneca applied many of the suggestions outlined by the theorists in an R&D process re-engineering activity (McNeil, 1996). They focused on three "major sequential phases: target identification, lead identification and lead optimization . . . This allowed Zeneca to arrive at its research target of developing six quality development candidates each year" (McNeil, 1996: 45). This approach is intended to focus the resources of Zeneca on a vital few compounds to secure the future of the company. In 1991, Merck & Co (then the most successful R&D based pharmaceutical company) did exactly the opposite. "To get 'megadrugs' flowing again, Merck & Co widened its scope of research from familiar targets such as cardiovascular disease to such areas as the central nervous system disorders and viral infections" (Weber, 1991). The shift in strategy, which included significant decentralization and development of autonomous R&D units, was considered essential at the time. This was because the centralized approach that they had previously developed was considered unwieldy and bureaucratic, and it slowed down the delivery of new compounds.

However, after three decades of empirical research into the management of the pharmaceutical R&D process "there still exists no precise prescription or recipe for successful innovation" (Rothwell, 1992: 223). The costs of research are increasing rapidly. An estimate made in 1987 (DiMasa *et al.*) of £150 million to bring a new chemical entity to market was updated in 1994 to £400 million (Lehman Brothers). Recent analysis published by PriceWaterhouse Coopers has projected falling returns from pharmaceutical companies unless R&D productivity is improved:

> Costs must be slashed. It is not possible to maintain total shareholder returns at [current] levels unless costs are driven back substantially . . . The challenge for the industry is increased because developments in genomics means that future medicines are likely to be suitable only for patients belonging to particular genotypes . . . potential market size [for each] will be correspondingly smaller.
>
> (Durman, 1998)

Notice how this literature focuses on control in which new product development is an intended and designed process in which risk is analyzed and uncertainty reduced. The expectation is of a new product trajectory that is stable, regular and predictable.

How the literature and the story match

It is common in the literature on organizations to argue that change within an organization is triggered by changes in the external environment. Managers are supposed to predict these environmental changes before they occur and take anticipatory action to meet them so that fit between the organization and its environment is restored.

Managers in a pharmaceutical business are supposed to observe and
analyze both their own organization and its environment so that they can
identify the variables to be controlled. The purpose is to increase the rate
of new product development from R&D pipelines so as to achieve
required rates of return on capital. This amounts to a belief that managers
can make the required choices independently of what others in the
industry are doing and so control their organization's destiny. This, quite
clearly, did not happen in the story recounted earlier in this chapter.
Instead, it seems to me that every move made by people in one
organization provoked moves in another in a continuous process, which
sometimes took on amplifying forms that no one could have foreseen.
Managers were often caught in interlocking patterns of belief that had
relatively little to do with objective reality. Let me explain why I hold this
view.

Following the success of Tagamet, stock market analysts began to believe
that SK&F had an approach to managing its R&D activities that was
fundamentally different from that of other companies. Managers at
SK&F began to believe this too. The stock market value of the company
increased dramatically, reflecting both rapid profit growth fuelled by
Tagamet and also future expectations around new compounds that would
flow in a predictable and controlled way from the research process in
place. Managers at all levels of the company began to believe that they
really did have the R&D process under control and began to behave
according to this belief. As a consequence, the company's R&D costs and
aspirations grew out of proportion to its underlying capabilities and more
in line with the expectations of the analysts and commentators. How
managers in the company made sense of the Tagamet success influenced
the analysts, who in turn influenced the managers, who then behaved as if
they knew what would happen, as if they had the right answer, which in
turn influenced the analysts even more. An amplifying process developed
in which the company and its environment were co-creating each other.
Managers at SK&F and at Glaxo also co-created an environment as the
former regularly increased the price of Tagamet attracting the latter to the
market with a rapid attack once Zantac was approved. Again, there was
an amplifying process of co-creation at work.

By 1982 the situation was bleaker and confidence in SK&F's
management was being undermined. Managers began to realize that they
did not, after all, possess a magic approach to research and so sought to
diversify the business in order to try to maintain profit flows and build
security for the future. This sudden switch in strategy caught the stock

market analysts by surprise. The bubble burst and the stock price lost some of its sheen. Meanwhile, executives continued to project a good future for pharmaceuticals; it was just going to take more time. Unanticipated shifts in US Government policy undermined the projected success of the Beckman purchase, which in turn undermined confidence in the management of SKB still further. So, deliberate steps taken to improve the perceived viability of the company had adverse consequences, contrary to those intended. Many consequences seem to have been totally outside the control of those managing the company.

SKB approached 1988 dependent on two major streams of earnings from Tagamet and Dyazide in the US and still with no new products emerging from its pipeline. We now know that at this time the teams at Beecham were analyzing the potential for companies with which to merge, as they struggled to achieve the growth they were looking for. However, although SKB featured on the Beecham list at that time "it was in sixth place as a possible partner because of its market capitalization" (Bauman et al., 1997: 54). This was to change dramatically in the space of a few weeks. Dyazide had come off patent in 1980, eight years previously. The US Food and Drug Administration (FDA) held off approving any generic products, encouraging SKB to develop a replacement product. In August 1987 they decided to change their position and approved a generic product for sale. SKB, having failed to take advantage of the situation offered to it by the FDA, was critically exposed and as a result of the FDA announcement lost £1 billion in market capitalization in one day.

In a bid to recover the situation, managers decided to advertise Tagamet in the national press for the first time. Unfortunately, the pre-established pattern of annual price rises triggered the trade (again outside of SKB's control) to stock up in anticipation of price increases and higher sales. This stock build-up pulled 25 percent of SKB's sales from 1988 into 1987. The net result of all this was to trigger a fall in the share price of the company, which placed the market capitalization of SKB in the range that the Beecham team regarded as reasonable. This triggered a discussion around a merger of equals. Potential for something new emerged from events which themselves emerged from unintended consequences of very deliberate management action. It was almost as if the harder the team at SKB tried to bring the situation under control and deliver consistent results, the faster it ran away from them.

Is it reasonable to believe managers can understand these processes sufficiently to anticipate their course and make them predictable? The story of how SKB arrived at the point of merger with Beecham does not seem to me to be consistent with the picture suggested by theorists who present research-based pharmaceutical companies as well-oiled machines. The story suggests to me that the main views presented in the literature are simply myths. Mainstream thinking about pharmaceutical innovations emphasize deliberate, dependable, successful, well-managed, highly productive and efficient innovative pharmaceutical R&D processes. The process of innovation is understood as one in which managers are "in control." If these myths indicate what should have been happening then all of us at SKB were incompetent and I do not believe that this was the case. It is the theories that are inadequate as explanations, not the practice of the managers involved. The theories are inadequate because they emphasize one pole of experience, namely, that to do with being "in control" in a situation characterized mainly by stability and predictability, the known. There is a much closer match between the SKB story and the explanations of those who focus attention on social and political processes (Kanter, 1984, 1988; Van de Ven, 1988) and the ambiguity they entail (Frost and Egri, 1991). However, even these perspectives seem to me to present an explanation that focuses on individual managers. They present explanations and prescriptions in which individual managers use, or should use, political processes in intentional, controlled ways to achieve what they have individually decided in advance to achieve.

For me, on the other hand, the story brings home the paradoxical situation in which practicing managers must live. The paradox is that managers are simultaneously "in control" of their business and yet "not in control." I am not arguing here that the business is out of control, but rather, that it is not controlled or controllable in the way that mainstream theories suggest. Moreover, the story suggests to me the need to think of R&D as transformative processes of communicative interaction, particularly communication in the form of ordinary everyday conversations between researchers as they go about their personally motivated search to become more successful scientists, and between them and managers in many parts of the business. A pharmaceutical business exemplifies, for me, the complex processes of self organization/emergence. Scientists struggle on a daily basis, in their own local situations, to make sense of disease states in the body, which is itself dynamic complex processes. They search for compounds that have some kind of therapeutic effect without serious detrimental side effects and frequently they find what they were not expecting to find. The timeframes involved mean that decisions made today will not be brought to commercial fruition for possibly eight to ten years, by which time the world will have moved on significantly as government policies and competitive conditions change. Indeed the company doing the research may no longer even exist. Product developments initiated today may well not be commercially viable when they come to fruition. Internal politics affect the development of products in many unexpected ways.

Yet alongside all this uncertainty, and in tension with it, there is the logic and discipline of basic scientific research as it grinds on through its rigorous routines, attempting to make objective sense of the world. The intentions of the scientists, driven to become the next James Black, are inextricably coupled to the personal ambitions of managers right up to the CEO who wants to prove his or her ability to deliver consistent growth, as demanded by stock market analysts. Products like Tagamet emerge as a success because of the commitment of many people acting in various, often conflicting ways. How products like Tagamet develop, and what kind of commercial success they later bring, are also highly dependent on what other people in supplier, customer, competitor and regulatory organizations are doing. Tagamet co-evolved with its market as people realized that it had become a possible cure for them and as competitors were attracted to the market that had been created. Tagamet was probably the most powerful trigger of change in the history of the company and this was in many ways unplanned. The research activity was planned in some senses but the intuition needed to get something meaningful from the initial compound synthesis could not be catered for in any plan. Neither could the ability of the research team to continue to argue for the continuation of its budget in the face of potential cuts. The company exploded into growth unforeseen by its managers and employees. In fact there were problems keeping up with the events that the product triggered. For six years SK&F had a monopoly in the field with the product. Given the way the product was developed, it was argued that SK&F could now surely apply the approach to other disease states and produce follow up compounds. It was not to be.

Nobody could have predicted the time-frames for the outcomes achieved. Nor could any one have predicted whether the mix in the development team was going to work or not. Black's experience had been in heart-related developments, not ulcers. The decisions about whether to fund the research or not, could easily have gone in favor of other projects. Black's decision to leave ICI and move to SK&F in 1964 potentially created the opportunity in SK&F rather than in ICI. Many individual choices intertwined to generate the outcome that emerged.

The story told in this chapter about management at the highest levels of the hierarchy is similar in many ways to that in the last chapter about management at the lowest hierarchical level. In my view, both reflect the paradox of control. The story of product development, marketing success and mergers cannot be told simply in terms of intention in relation to known, predictable situations. An adequate account for what happened has to include the responses evoked and provoked by others and the uncertainty, indeed unknowability, of many aspects of the situations in which people were interacting in their various organizations. The literature, however, presents explanations primarily in terms of intention and certainty, while largely ignoring their opposites. In practice, however, it is these simultaneously present opposites with which managers must live. It is this lack of congruence between the focus of attention of mainstream thinking about management and the lived experience of managing that calls for an alternative explanation.

In fact new products and strategic directions emerge: drawing analogies from the complexity sciences

The SKB story told in this chapter seems to me to exemplify the kind of amplifying co-evolving processes that complexity scientists are seeking to understand. Others have also suggested that analogies from the complexity sciences are helpful in understanding the evolution of organizations and industries (e.g. Stacey, 1996; Marion, 1999; Stacey *et al.*, 2000).

The complexity sciences include the theories of chaos, dissipative structures, synergetics and complex adaptive systems. What they all have in common is an interest in modeling and explaining the evolution of highly interactive non-linear systems and processes. They seek to model and explain phenomena that display the internal capacity to spontaneously produce coherence in the absence of any blueprint, external designer or internal controller. A central concept is that of self organization and emergence. Self organization is the process of entities interacting with each other on the basis of their own local organizing principles in the absence of any overall blueprint or program. What the complexity sciences demonstrate is that such self-organizing processes produce coherent patterns that emerge in interaction rather than being programmed before the interaction. I do not intend here to discuss the complexity sciences in any detail. That has been done in the first volume of this series, which discusses a number of different strands of thinking in the complexity sciences and explores how they are being used to understand human action in organizations (Stacey *et al.*, 2000). What I will do here is point to how the suggestions made in that first volume might be used to make sense of the story told in this chapter about SmithKline Beckman. In the rest of this section I want to draw on the discussion by Stacey, Griffin and Shaw of analogies for organizations provided by Kauffman's (1993, 1995a) development of the notion of "fitness landscapes."

Fitness landscapes

The idea of a "fitness landscape" was suggested as a metaphor for biological evolution (Wright, 1931) in which the evolution of sets of genes (species) is thought of as movement across a landscape consisting of peaks and valley. A peak represents a fit set of genes, that is, one that is highly adapted to its environment and the higher the peak the more fit is the set of genes, or species. A valley represents an evolutionary disaster, that is, very low levels of fitness and the lower the valley the less the probability of survival. Evolution is then understood as a hill climbing process, that is, movement out of valleys and up towards the highest peak. In biological evolution, this process is one of trial and error in which chance variations in individual genes in a particular set (a species) are thought of as a move on the landscape. Natural selection weeds out the downward moves and keeps evolution moving towards peaks, with periodic disasters or tumbles into valleys along the way. By analogy, an organization can be thought of as a set of strategies, for example, new product developments and mergers. However, instead of thinking of strategies evolving through chance mutation, as in biology, they are thought of, in mainstream literature, as the choices managers make. The aim is to move an organization out of fitness valleys (losses) and up fitness peaks (profit). By analogy, one could also think of the evolution of a population of organizations, for example the pharmaceutical industry, as an adaptive walk across a fitness landscape.

The complexity scientist, Kauffman, has used this concept to explore the dynamics of evolution using computer simulations of fitness landscapes (1995a). The shape of the landscape, that is, whether it has few high peaks or many low peaks, determines how easy or difficult it is for a species (organization) to reach a fit state.

A very rugged landscape with large numbers of low peaks makes it difficult to find a reasonably good state of fitness simply by following the hill-climbing rule because that rule so easily leads to being trapped on a low peak. In his simulations, Kauffman shows that a very rugged landscape results when entities comprising a species (or organization) are highly interconnected. This is because connections create the constraint of having to respond. When they are connected, one entity must act in response to the actions of others it is connected to. If an entity is connected to two others and they each call for a different response, then it has to handle two conflicting constraints. It follows that the greater the number of connections, the more the potential conflict in the constraints that entities create for each other. The more the conflicting constraints to be accommodated, the more rugged the landscape and the more easily a species (or organization) is trapped on a low peak. In competition with others, sets of entities with low fitness will experience waves of extinction. The dynamic is, therefore, one of instability.

However, when entities comprising a species (organization) are only sparsely connected, then conflicting constraints will be minimal and the fitness landscape will be rather smooth, with a small number of very high peaks, that is, a small number of very good survival strategies that are easy to find. This kind of landscape implies a stable evolutionary path for a single species (organization) taken on its own. However, this kind of landscape also makes it easy for competitors to find the same survival strategy so that none can hold onto competitive advantage for long, leading to waves of destruction for the population of species (organizations) taken together.

When entities in a species (organization) are neither too richly nor too sparsely interconnected, then the fitness landscape will be rugged but not too rugged. Conflicting constraints will be neither too numerous nor too few so that the species (organization) is neither too stable nor too unstable. When this dynamic prevails, evolution is not characterized by large waves of large extinction events. Instead evolution proceeds with new species appearing alongside small numbers of large extinctions and large numbers of small extinctions. This pattern of destruction is known as the power law and it imparts relative control to the pattern of evolution. While no agent is "in control" of the system's evolution, it is nevertheless evolving in a controlled manner and the source of this control lies in the pattern of conflicting constraints. This dynamic, represented by landscapes that are neither too rugged (unstable) nor too smooth (stable), is known as the "edge of chaos."

The dynamic of complex interactions, however, does not depend on the nature of interaction within one species or organization alone. One species or organization is connected to others and so they have to cooperate and compete with each other in order to survive. They co-evolve and this means that they deform each other's fitness landscapes. The number of species in an ecology (organizations in an industry) and connections between them determine how much they deform each other's landscapes. Broadly speaking, when species (organizations) are simple, their numbers small and connections between them are sparse, then there is little deformation of landscapes, that is, the pattern of evolution is stability. However, the landscape keeps heaving about, the pattern of co-evolution is chaotic, when large numbers of complex species (organizations) are highly interconnected. At some intermediate point between these conditions, the dynamic of the edge of chaos arises. Kauffman argues that there is a self-organizing tendency for the process of evolution to evolve to the "edge of chaos" for it is there that the potential for the emergence of novelty lies.

So, the dynamic experienced by a single species (organization) is not simply determined by its own nature alone but also by the nature of the larger process it is part of. In other words, the "choice" open to any single species or organization is highly limited and this insight significantly challenges the taken-for-granted assumption that managers can choose strategic directions for their organization. Such choice is highly limited because every organization is in interaction with others and together they co-create the emergent dynamics of their interaction. Each makes choices, trying to influence outcomes and the dynamics in which those outcomes emerge, but outcomes emerge from the conflicting constraints they create for each other, not the simple choice of any one of them. The dynamics of the interaction cause themselves as the populations of species (organizations) spontaneously evolve to the edge of chaos.

In this theory, the operation of competitive selection depends upon the internal dynamic of the evolving species (organization), that is, upon the self-organizing interaction between the entities of which it is composed. The fitness landscape, as a metaphor for the dynamic or pattern of evolution, is being constructed by the properties of interaction. The internal dynamic is one of enabling cooperation and of conflicting constraints at the same time, a paradoxical dynamic of simultaneous cooperation and competition. Connections between agents may be taken as analogous to relationships between people and relationships immediately constrain those in relationship. Power is constraint and conflicting constraints, therefore, translate, in human terms, to power relations. In other words, the emerging strategies of an organization may be caused by the nature of power relations between its members, between it and other organizations, by chance and by competitive selection. This is a view of causality in which power and conflict, inevitably intertwined with cooperation, are fundamental to the emergence of coherence. No agent within the species or organization is choosing the pattern of evolution and neither is anyone outside it. Instead, that pattern emerges in the interaction between the entities, neither by chance nor by choice alone, but through the capacity to produce coherence that is intrinsic to interaction itself.

The implications of this argument are very important, namely, that the evolution of an industry and the evolution of the strategies of an organization within it, is not caused by the choices of individual managers in one organization taken on its own but by the nature of interaction, relationship, cooperation and competition between people in each organization and between organizations. The dynamics of individual organizations simultaneously form, and are formed by, the dynamics of the industry. This perspective is a direct challenge to the mainstream notion that managers choose what happens to their organization as a whole and so should be lauded when the organization succeeds and denigrated when it fails.

Causality

This perspective points to an understanding of causality that is very different to that underlying the theory of strategic choice. Stacey, Griffin and Shaw (2000) have called this alternative understanding of causality "transformative teleology," in which interaction is seen as being under perpetual construction moving toward an unpredictable future (Prigogine, 1997; Prigogine and Stengers, 1985). The process of construction is that of forming and being formed at the same time and it produces repetitive patterns always with the potential for transformation. Here species (organizations) change as they interact with one another. They co-evolve, with one living in niches afforded by the actions of others. For example, flowers co-evolved with the insects that pollinated them and fed on their nectar. Host–parasite systems co-evolve too. The agent of malaria alters its surface antigens to evade detection by the host, while in its turn the host immune system evolves to destroy the malaria. This is the notion of co-evolution and one that is important to explore because it underpins thinking about emergence. In Kauffman's words:

> the attractors of the adaptive process are local optima which are single points. In a 'co-evolutionary process', however, the adaptive landscape of one actor heaves and deforms as the other adaptors make their own adaptive moves. Thus co-evolving behavior is in no way limited to attaining point attractors which are local optima, nor is it even clear that co-evolving systems must be optimizing anything whatsoever.
>
> (Kauffman, 1993: 238)

Kauffman describes the co-evolutionary effect in relation to economics through the example of the car.

> When the car came in, it drove out the horse. With the horse went the smithy, the stable, the saddlery, the harness shop, buggies, and the Pony Express. But once cars are around, it makes sense to expand the oil industry, build gas stations, and pave the roads. Once the roads are paved, people drive everywhere, so motels are useful. When cars get faster, traffic lights, traffic cops, and parking fines make their way into the economy and our behavior patterns.
>
> (Kauffman, 1995b: 126)

Co-evolution, as a process, can be seen in the context of evolutionary biology, economics and the development of companies, and also in the very nature of the process of human interaction. Marion (1999) uses the fitness landscape analogy to explain the development of the personal computer industry.

Similarly, SK&F was clearly not a company on an isolated search of its own, but was affected by other companies or communities engaged in their searches. Its fitness landscape was defined not only by its own strategies but also by those of others. The main point here is that as one company, working in a similar economic niche to others, succeeds in developing something new so it changes both its own landscape and that of others. This impact may spill outside of its niche too as every individual company landscape is interconnected with others and so the whole situation is in effect a heaving, ever-changing, never-ceasing interdependent process. Equally, it is not a question of these landscapes being mapped out and it being a choice of which to pursue. The choices made by individuals in their companies become reflected in some way in the emergence of their company's strategy which in turn impacts and affects others in a way which occurs as each makes sense of the other's actions. The whole interactive process is evolving in an unpredictable manner such that one cannot look forward in order to determine where the potential outcomes lie. In addition, it is not a preconceived future. It becomes as it happens. It is not already there. It appears as it is co-created.

The story of SK&F highlights this well. The choice Black's team made to set up an insurance policy in the form of the histamine research program was an incident that created the opportunity for SK&F, which created the opportunity for the treatment of ulcers with a drug. Not only did this impact the landscape for SK&F but also that of Glaxo and its development of Zantac, which in turn fuelled the funding that enabled the company to buy Wellcome, which in turn enabled the possibility of a merger in 1998 between SB and Glaxo/Wellcome as well as impacting the lives (and landscapes) of many millions of employees, shareholders, patients and so on. It is impossible to describe all the impacts, of course. However, the heaving landscape model appears to make sense of what evolved.

There is nobody or nothing "in control." At the level of the landscape nobody is, or can be, in control. The story of SK&F/SKB's development, understood through the fitness landscape analogy, points to how fragile the notion of being in control is. While managers have some sense of being in control, nowhere is this actually the case. It is not possible here to demonstrate control being achieved. What can be seen, in hindsight only, are patterns that appear to be coherent and to make sense. These patterns seem to be of an emergent and self-organized nature driven by intentional acts of people who intend certain outcomes but never quite experience what they thought they would. What we see is behavior that is controlled even though no one is in control of it.

Allen argues that: "Change can mean simply a change in the quantities of the different variables present initially or change can refer to qualitative change where new types of artifact, actor (business, sector, individual or organization) can appear over time" (1998: 47). Observation, analysis and attempts to determine the key variables that would give control over the R&D process require the construction of an abstract model including the critical variables. This thinking is an extrapolation of that used to predict the next events in physical systems. The "problem" with this approach is that a system with non-linear interactions between its micro-elements can "undergo symmetry breaking instabilities, and hence exhibit qualitative change in which new dimensions emerge in the attribute space necessary to characterize its behavior" (Allen, 1998: 49).

In other words, the interaction of the system's micro-components – in an R&D organization this means the interactions between the people working together – may lead them to create new meanings. This, in turn, might lead them to act in ways that could not have been predicted from previously established patterns of success. According to Allen this highlights a problem: "usual methods which have proved so powerful in dealing with physical systems, seem only capable of saying that prediction is possible in systems involving living things, but only if nothing much really changes" (Allen, 1998: 49). From a complexity perspective, serial cause and effect notions are too simplistic, and an organization would be thought of as co-evolving with its environment. This view leads to an important shift in the way one thinks about control: the more interconnected a company and its environment are, the less control its managers have.

Conclusion

Shareholders and analysts expect the CEO to be in control of the business. The CEO expects his business unit managers to be in control of their business units and they expect their subordinate managers to be in control of their areas of responsibility. "In control" means producing consistent results in line with expectations and equal to, or better than, similar companies in the same industry.

In the pharmaceutical industry, one of the fundamental drivers of success is the delivery of novel therapies for disease conditions that threaten or reduce the quality of life. The inherent nature of the innovation appears to be that of self-organizing, sense-making processes of conversation between those engaged in particular research projects. The particular product story reviewed, Tagamet, has been described as a case study in rational drug development. In one sense this is true, in that the approach was logical and rational. In another sense, however, it is not true. Intuitive guesses and actions were intertwined with the logical, analytical approach. While it is possible in some ways to control whether money is spent in a particular area, there is no way that the outcomes intended can be controlled. The future cash flows and consistency of results in this company were critically dependent on processes that were inherently uncontrollable.

The fortunes of SK&F overall seem to have been dictated in many ways by events that were influenced but not controlled by management teams.

Intentional actions taken "inside" the company triggered unintended consequences "outside" it, which in turn triggered further actions, having both intended and unintended consequences. This is a co-evolutionary process.

I have argued that mainstream literature on product development does not provide explanations that resonate with this experience. They present, I think, a one-sided view that collapses the paradoxical nature of organizational and industrial evolution to one pole, namely, that of being "in control." The literature talks of intention forming the future direction of an organization, a direction toward a largely known, predictable future. The experience, however, requires an explanation that retains the paradox, that is, the tension of responses evoked and provoked as well as action intended; movement toward a future that is known and unknown, predictable and unpredictable at the same time. I have suggested that an explanation in terms of complex responsive processes built on analogies from the complexity sciences does retain the paradoxical experience of managing. The notion of the dynamic at the "edge of chaos" is one of paradox, that is, of patterns of change that are stable and unstable, predictable and unpredictable at the same time. A complex responsive process theory of the evolution of organizations is built on a notion of causality in which the future is under perpetual construction by the interactions of people in an organization and by interactions between organizations. The future is perpetually constructed as continuity and transformation at the same time. This theory refocuses attention away from the choices of individual managers and organizations and toward the nature of their relationships with each other. It suggests that the capacity for spontaneous transformation is intrinsic to interaction itself.

The question now is just how this transformative co-evolutionary process occurs and just what the role of intentional action is in this process. In other words, the question is just how managers live with the paradox of being in control and not being in control at the same time. To explore this question, I want to turn to my own direct experience of changes in SB at the time of the merger.

4 Managing in a post-merger situation

- ◈ **What the literature has to say on mergers**
- ◈ **Coping with the post-merger situation at SmithKline Beecham**
- ◈ **Networking**

The last chapter recounted some of the key events leading up to the merger between SmithKline Beckman and Beecham to create the new company of SmithKline Beecham (SB). That chapter explored how one might make sense of these events. I argued that mainstream thinking about the strategic development of an organization, including new product development, is based on the assumption that managers are by and large "in control" of such developments. This thinking, however, does not resonate with my experience of these events because that experience was characterized as much by features of "not being in control" as it was by features to do with "being in control." It is difficult to make sense of this fundamentally paradoxical experience in terms of a way of thinking that collapses the paradox to one of its poles, namely, that of "being in control." This led me to suggest an alternative way of thinking, which employs analogies from the complexity sciences that may be more helpful in making sense of my experience because it is a way of thinking in which paradox is central. From this alternative perspective, the merger between the two companies emerged in the ongoing interactions between individual managers, and various groups of managers, over a number of years preceding the merger itself. The intentions and choices of powerful managers certainly played a part, and in that sense they were "in control." But these intentions themselves emerged in previous interactions. They constituted gestures and the unpredictable responses that they evoked and provoked, and their reactions to these responses, also played a powerful role. In these senses they were "not in control."

In this chapter, I turn to the story of how my colleagues and I carried out our management roles in the situation immediately following the announcement of the merger. Before coming to the story of my own experience I want to look briefly at what the literature on mergers might lead me to expect in post-merger situations and what it has to say about how managers should conduct themselves in such situations.

What the literature has to say on mergers

When I turn to the literature on post-merger situations, I immediately notice how most of it is concerned with top management motives for undertaking mergers and acquisitions and their roles in subsequent processes of integration. The concern is with the factors leading to success and, therefore, with the prescriptions for the successful management of post-merger and post-acquisition situations. Motives are described in terms of business strategies and shareholder value maximization (e.g. Halpern, 1983; Mueller, 1977). Key success factors and the prescriptions for realizing them are identified as follows:

- People with good attitudes towards their jobs and their organizations are likely to view a merger more positively (Costello *et al.*, 1963) and so enhance the chances of it being successful. To sustain good attitudes and reduce anxiety, mergers should, therefore, be well planned and well communicated (Shirley, 1977; Marks, 1982).
- Attitude surveys in post-merger/acquisition situations (e.g. Schweiger *et al.*, 1987) point to causes of post-merger problems to do with people feeling a loss of identity and competence, experiencing anxiety, obsession with survival and a lack of information, and having to cope with family repercussions. The conclusion is then drawn that

> not enough was done in the acquired organization to deal with problems caused by the acquisition . . . It became apparent that there had been little preplanning for human resource issues. Even when employees were considered, management faced so much uncertainty and ambiguity about the future that they were not always clear about what actions needed to be taken and by whom.
>
> (133)

The implication is that managers should meet increased dependency needs of employees: "it is important for managers to take the lead . . . a manager who takes control of his or her personal situation can be very effective" (136).

- The role of the manager in post-merger/acquisition activities is to return the organization to a "state of equilibrium" by establishing a new vision for all so as to reduce uncertainty about the direction of the new company: "the implicit stability of Purpose, Power, and People that exists in most organizations has been upset. Many inexperienced acquirers ignore their first key task: restoring and communicating a new equilibrium in the '3Ps'" (Balloun and Gridley, 1990: 91).
- Furthermore, "basic decisions must be made and communicated quickly about the top-level power structure, and about the basic philosophy and timing for post merger actions. Realism about where power lies is advisable – there are few true mergers of equals" (Balloun and Gridley, 1990: 94).
- Also, "reducing ambiguity and uncertainty for people at all levels is always a critical requirement" (Balloun and Gridley 1990: 94). This leads to prescriptions to do with better formal internal communications about the merger or acquisition (Bastien, 1987; Perry, 1986); effective changes in organizational structure (Mirvis, 1985); and the meshing of different cultures (Buono and Bowditch, 1989; McManus and Hergert, 1988).
- Concern is expressed about productive work time lost in gossiping about a merger (Wishard, 1985; Cabrera, 1985). This leads to calls for understanding patterns of absenteeism, staff turnover and poor performance (Napier, 1989).
- Concern is also expressed about the reaction of middle managers and their possible psychological withdrawal from their work due to feelings of helplessness, ascribed to "the belief that the terminated employees were treated unfairly and the loss of job control . . . Further, both helplessness and the belief that the terminated employees were treated unfairly were positively related to the surviving managers' perception that the newly merged corporation was detrimental to their career development needs" (Fried et al., 1996: 422). The prescriptions are: practices to deal with potential stress experienced by survivors of mergers/acquisitions; restoring job control; developing systematic communication patterns to "enhance employees' confidence in the future career prospects of the merged corporation" (422).

The literature, therefore, focuses on rational processes of planning, communication and the rapid establishment of order to remove the mess and anxiety of the merger/acquisition experience. The prescriptions are aimed at containing and managing uncertainty so as to deliver specified outcomes. Again, the literature highlights the "in control" aspect of a post-merger situation and deals with the opposites by advocating the removal of all aspects representing "not in control." The emphasis is on the formal, legitimate structures and procedures. But is what they propose possible? Does this kind of perspective help a manager trying to cope with post-merger situations? In answer to these questions I now turn to my own post-merger experience.

Coping with the post-merger situation at SmithKline Beecham

Back at the factory in Welwyn Garden City where I was working as a manager of manufacturing operations, geographically and hierarchically distant from the events described in the last chapter, the announcement of the merger was met with disbelief, quickly followed by great anxiety about the future. All our plans, both business and personal, seemed to dissolve rapidly in the uncertainty and it felt as if we had lost control of our destinies. Individuals spontaneously began to position themselves to get the best out of the situation, personally and for their families. I had been planning to make a significant change in my life by moving into marketing. The merger, therefore, offered me an opportunity and so I felt a mixture of excitement and anxiety. The emotional responses of others were varied and many working relationships changed significantly. There was a sense that what was solid prior to the merger had become much less solid as a result of the merger announcement. The previous patterns of relationship, which had held us together before, were not of much use in the new context. We were now in unmapped territory and had to invent what we did next. In other words, we experienced very much what the literature describes in other merger and acquisition situations. As described in the previous chapter strenuous efforts were made, as recommended in the literature, to communicate and lay down guidelines for how post-merger decisions were to be taken in a rational, planned manner, putting emotion and personal ambition to one side. There was a genuine desire to restore order as rapidly as possible and action was taken on this desire, as recommended in the literature. But what actually happened?

Post-merger planning for the UK pharmaceutical subsidiary in 1989

Immediately after the merger, I was invited, along with a number of other managers from head office functions and various production sites, to join a business development group, which met in the UK headquarters of the newly formed SmithKline Beecham. None of us had foreseen the major change that had just overtaken us, but now in mid-1989 we were required to produce a three-year plan to 1992 for the UK business unit that had just been formed. The purpose of the exercise was to enable the UK subsidiary to move into the future along a path chosen by its top management team, within the direction laid down by the corporation's top executives. The goal they set for 1992 was to maintain a position in the top five pharmaceutical companies in the UK.

To carry out our task, we first had to make some kind of sense of what was happening in the corporation and, in particular, we had to identify the new drug developments coming to fruition because they would be the main driver of our profit growth. In the last chapter, I described the prospects for the SKB product portfolio just before the merger was announced, giving subsequent outcomes in brackets. Of course, at the time of the planning exercise, we did not know these outcomes and so we had to plan on the basis of projections made in July 1989 by the R&D teams in both of the original companies. We also had to make judgments about likely market developments over the next three to five years. Against the background of these judgments, we then had to make projections of the sales we would need to meet our market share objective, to be compared with the sales we expected to achieve.

In order to do this, we developed a business model, which assumed that the announced commitments from R&D would be realized; that inflation would run at an average of around 6 percent; that the UK Government policies on the pharmaceutical industry would remain broadly the same; that growth for competing companies would be more or less in line with previous trends unless they were affected by a product coming off patent. Applying the model to the baseline of ethical pharmaceutical sales by SmithKline Beckman in the UK amounting to £150 million in 1988, ranked second after Glaxo, we determined that we needed to achieve a sales position of something around £200 million in 1992 to meet our market share objective. We then took the new product projections from the R&D group and generated forecasts for the following five-year period for our own product range. We focused on the product mix for 1992 and estimated the contributions to sales from the new products to be introduced. Having done this, and taken into account the sales we expected to lose as a result of Tagamet coming off patent, we estimated that the target was achievable provided that we got the new products from R&D.

As we developed our spreadsheets and cash flow projections we became very taken with the models of the world we had built. Our thinking was channeled into tweaking what we knew rather than considering the possibility of the world completely changing and the UK Government introducing a limited list with half our products on it, for example. Never did we think that something radically different might happen. Small, incremental tweaks were all we could envisage. There were so many possibilities that it was pointless trying to take account of all of them. So, we automatically limited the possibilities. It was as if, in order to cope with the uncertainty of not knowing, we constructed even better analyses of what we had wedded our thoughts to, in an attempt to convince ourselves that we were right and that our scenario for the future was a valid one.

The more the analysis seemed to make sense to us, as we grasped at every hint of confirmation, the more we developed the story of the potential future we had mapped out for the business. "Our goal is to become a top five UK Pharmaceutical Company by 1992" became our sales pitch to the corporate management team. "We will achieve this by launching new compounds as we receive them from R&D, coupled with some strategic acquisitions in the vaccine area to shift the emphasis into the traveler market, which we feel is as yet untapped." Projections of sales and profits over the plan period became powerful tools in our presentations as we convinced ourselves, and those reviewing our plans, that we had a valid approach. Risks associated with key elements of the plan were perhaps under-emphasized in statements, for example, about the low risk of R&D missing delivery projections. It is relatively easy to become wedded to the logic of plans when one is deeply involved in developing them. They somehow take on a kind of solidness all on their own. Once the numbers are written down, the underlying assumptions seem to get lost in the background. Reviews usually revolve around the trends in the numbers, which always seem more solid than the real life situation. We really did believe that we would be able to pull off the new future for the UK business that we envisaged with a high degree of certainty. That belief helped to make us articulate and credible as we described it to others. After all, in our experience, the UK business had grown strongly for years as a result of the Tagamet success and the forward planning exercise had always indicated a gap between the profit target requested by the corporate team and the planned profit. However, every year something happened to close the gap so that target performance levels were achieved.

This plan was no exception to that previous pattern! When 1992 arrived, however, ten of the eleven product introductions did not materialize, amounting to a £38 million shortfall in the sales projection. But then there were also unexpected, yet significant, favorable swings in other products. The vaccines portfolio, for example, did not shrink as expected but continued to grow significantly. Also, the hepatitis A vaccine was launched in 1991 and contributed millions on the sales front. Furthermore, Engerix B sales did not decline as projected. Sales of Seroxat turned out to be three times the original projections in its first year. The resulting net sales amounted to approximately £190 million, achieving the goal of staying in the top five ranking, but not at all in the way that we had envisaged back in 1989.

We cannot say, therefore, that we achieved the goal because of the plan. This becomes even more evident when it is realized that we were making our plans without knowing what the cost structures would be because factories were yet to be rationalized. We could not know what form the rationalization would take because we were still trying to decide what it should be. But, if we were not really determining our future in this planning exercise, then what were we doing?

Making sense of post-merger planning

The kind of planning exercise we were engaged in can be understood in a number of different ways. For some it means taking the future into account in some way and laying out action in advance. In our planning, we certainly were trying to look ahead. However, in doing so, we were very much constrained by views of the world we were comfortable with. We took comfort from a picture that was more of the same, with a place in it for us. Others see planning as controlling the future (Ackoff, 1970) or creating controlled change in the environment (Ozbekhan, 1969: 152). In trying to think about the future, then, managers are also trying to gain some degree of control, to steer the organization they are part of. This is my sense of what we thought we were doing in the business development group. However, there was so much we did not know. We did not know how new product developments would fare. We did not know what competitors would do in response to the merger. We did not even know what we would be doing to rationalize production and so alter our cost structure. Nevertheless we proceeded as if we did know; as if we could stay "in control."

As Mintzberg points out: "An obsession with control generally seems to reflect a fear of uncertainty. We all fear uncertainty to some degree, and one way to deal with a felt lack of control, to ensure no surprises, is to flip over – to seek control over anything that might surprise us . . . In a sense reducing uncertainty is the profession of planners" (1994: 202–3). I see the planning exercise we carried out in 1989 very much as a form of defense against the anxiety of dealing with the uncertainty facing us. It gave us the basis for action that we wanted to take and acted like a container for our concerns and energies. The emergent nature of our lives produces anxieties, which we need to find some way of controlling in order to act.

Planning and goal-oriented behavior appears to be linked to the containment of anxiety associated with uncertainty about the future. To some degree the plans and projections made at the UK business unit level gave us, as individuals, a sense of control over our own destiny. I suggest that this had a great deal to do with achieving a sense of control over future events in order to give confidence to those concerned so that they could act into what was really an open ended and highly uncertain future. The strong influence of previously useful patterns that were associated with success seemed to lead to projections based on the same into the future. My reflection now leads me to understand that the "felt" control and confidence derived from it was misplaced. Plans and projections for new products did not come to fruition. While "in control" of internal events, as a team we were caught off guard by external events beyond our working environment. In a sense we ended up trying, very efficiently, to climb Ben Nevis when the true prize lay at the top of Mount Everest on a continent we did not even appreciate existed! We did what the literature recommends. All the words to do with being "in control" featured in our conversations: intention, design, certainty, predictability, and so on. However, the subjective experience was characterized just as much by the words to do with "not being in control," namely, responding, not knowing, unpredictability, and so on. And this vague perception of not being in control triggered anxiety, which we unconsciously had to find a way of dealing with.

I have already mentioned that our planning exercise proceeded without knowing what our cost structures would be because production in the two combined companies was to be rationalized. I will now describe something of how that rationalization took place in the UK in the months following the planning exercise.

Factory rationalization

Just before the merger, as I have already mentioned, I felt the need for a move and so I lobbied for a position in the marketing group, which I was offered. After the merger, towards the end of 1989, I started to prepare for the move but then Peter Black, production director at Welwyn, came to see me. He said "Phil, I want you to postpone your move to UK marketing for three months and work with me on UK factory integration activities for the merger. Don't worry about the marketing group. I've clarified and agreed this with them. They will hold open their offer to you until we have finished the project work we need to do." I was both taken aback and excited. I had worked hard to get the offer from marketing and was reluctant to give up the opportunity. However, Peter Black had decided that he needed me to support him and had convinced the marketing manager to postpone my move. There was not much I could do. On the other hand, I was curious and could see that the rationalization project might make a difference. So, I went quietly, never to return to the promised marketing position!

Peter explained that we would be part of a team that would look at the UK production operations of both SmithKline and Beecham and that we had to propose a combined UK production unit, which might or might not involve reducing the number of facilities. My role would be to support the team in its work. We would be a combined SmithKline and Beecham team led by a Beecham director, Bob Allen. Apparently, there was no prescribed outcome in the merger plans for factory rationalization and the team would have the task of recommending the way forward for the newly formed company in the UK.

Over the next few days Peter and I met several times. At first I felt he would know what to do; after all he was the production director. It was clear that he wanted the Welwyn factory to continue to operate in the new company, but otherwise he was open to many potential outcomes. Our discussions focused on the approach that the team should adopt in order to tackle the task. This was the first time I had ever been involved in a situation like this. Perhaps because I thought I would be leaving production, I took a slightly different view to Peter about the Welwyn factory. I believed that we should begin with an open mind about which, if any, of the factories should close. I felt loyalty to the business overall and wanted an open evaluation of the situation. I had been contributing to the development of the Welwyn factory for eight years and felt that the site would be successful if it was efficient. However, I did have loyalties to Peter. As we continued talking, it became clear that Peter wanted to bias the team's work so as to keep Welwyn operating. I was torn. I felt that we should be looking at the total cost of operating post-merger and deliver for the shareholders. In a sense we reached a compromise. The team process put forward enabled multiple outcomes to be reached.

Once we had developed proposals for the approach we also discussed how to sell them to the team when it first met. We discussed how we could influence the McKinsey consultant who would be supporting us. One of my tasks in these first few days was to evaluate the approach being advocated by McKinsey. This was a model derived from their experience with SK&F Canada when they rationalized their production operations in 1988. When we reviewed this, though, we realized that we would have to put forward a more relevant country-oriented approach.

Peter was gearing up to use any means at his disposal to keep the Welwyn factory in the picture. He had invested many years of his life creating one of the best pharmaceutical operations in the UK. Those that represented the threat were the consultants from McKinsey and the Beecham management team responsible for running the Beecham UK factory operations. In our preparation, then, we were seeking to exert the maximum control over the process in order to ensure the best outcome from a local viewpoint.

Lunch before the meeting

A meeting of the merger team was set up in London at the old Beecham headquarters, now renamed SB House. Suitably prepared, Peter Black and I drove together to the meeting. One of our intentions was to ascertain the position of the others. When we arrived we were taken to the private dining area – there were a number of tiers of dining in the old Beecham organization – to meet with the rest of the group. I remember it vividly. Director of UK Consumer Production Operations Derek King was the most senior Beecham person in the room and he told us that his position merited this private dining room, with its silver service routine. It had taken years to get to such a position, but now it was worth it. At Welwyn in the old SKB business, we had no such trappings. There was one canteen and everybody ate in it, including our managing director. The other Beecham executive present was Albert Peters, works controller at their Crawley site.

The atmosphere at this first meeting was strange for me, cold and somehow false. Each person introduced himself in terms of his position. Titles abounded and it seemed to me that each overplayed his relative importance. Almost immediately a pecking order was established. I was clearly at the bottom and Peter was clearly not at the top! This was unexpressed but it felt important. Peter's perception of his own worth and, therefore, influence in the team, was critically important. Technically he was highly qualified and intellectually he was a winner, but politically he was not well connected, so in that sense all the preparations for our approach to the team were not going to influence the outcome much. We immediately knew this. Over lunch, there was no discussion about the business at all or about the task we had to carry out.

Looking back, the point at which this group of four men met in London for the first time turned out to be critical. All of the agendas came together in the room, including our prepared process, developed in the hope of significantly influencing the outcome in favor of Welwyn. Yet, even as we greeted each other, it was as if the potential outcomes were limiting themselves. An unconscious patterning process seemed to be operating in the initial exchanges. How did this pattern establish itself so rapidly? There seemed to be an implicit patterning of power relations in the initial welcome, which established a pecking order. I am sure that my feelings about the pecking order affected my behavior, and the same probably applied to the others. At this point I felt that the ultimate outcome would be the closure of Welwyn, no matter how much Peter wanted us to argue otherwise. I think the rapid emergence of a particular pattern of power relations between us had to do with an already existing, influential network of Beecham executives. Beecham's production operations in the UK were organized into a consumer division (three production facilities), headed by Derek King, and a pharmaceuticals division (four facilities), headed by Hal Jackson, to whom Albert Peters reported. Hal had encouraged Albert to go to Crawley a year earlier and the two had a close working relationship. Derek and Albert, therefore, brought with them a web of powerful relationships, which could be sensed even if it was not discussed. There was no global head of operations in SK&F and Peter represented only the Welwyn production site. I was a rather junior member of the team.

Then there were the personal factors. Albert was a very ambitious person driven to build his career and prepared to take risks in order to succeed. Peter was getting towards the end of his career with the option of taking early retirement a distinct possibility so he could go painting in France;

something he often professed a desire to do. These motives, expressed guardedly in the conversation, affected the development of the group. As we eyed each other up, it was like some kind of primitive dance. Each made sense of himself in this new context. We definitely connected, verbally, at the surface level only. The process that Peter and I had worked out was accepted as reasonable in that it fitted the overall context. We would all look good putting this forward as the way to proceed. Peter was happy because he knew that he could influence the process and Albert was pleased because he could see he could influence it too.

The meeting

After lunch, we began to discuss the scope of the project and our work plan. There was some debate about the size of the cost reduction required from this project. This seemed to be the criterion according to which our success would be judged but it was far from clear. "What does one plus one equal?" was the question. "Is it 1.75, 1.5 or what?" In a sense we were looking for a context in which to place our efforts.

The discussion continued about the nature of the team process. Here, Peter succeeded in convincing the team that our proposals on how to proceed were good ones and that my role should be to collect the data for our work. It felt to me as if there were many undercurrents in the discussion. It turned out that the Beecham pharmaceuticals and consumer businesses were run almost totally separately. Derek King, from the consumer division, put forward his most important factory, St. Helens, as a candidate for analysis. I got the distinct impression (confirmed afterwards) that the old Beecham pharmaceutical management team had been trying for years to have the viability of St. Helens examined. I sensed there was a bigger game afoot; some of the non-verbal cues I picked up led me later into a discussion with Albert Peters about his views on the exercise. We agreed on the work plan mechanics; I would develop a product database and information would be provided to me.

Peter was fairly pleased with the meeting. As we drove back to Welwyn he reckoned that we had plenty of work to do but that the way the process had been set up would put us in a good position to deliver a positive result for Welwyn. The premise was that both he and Albert Peters would be able to create a situation where consumer production could be transferred into the pharmaceutical sites of Welwyn and Crawley from St.

Helens. They seemed convinced that the cost of converting St. Helens to meet the quality requirements for pharmaceutical production would rule out any transfers from either Welwyn or Crawley. I was concerned to put the facts and data forward so that we could look at the whole picture before making judgments.

Developing the options

Over the following week we produced a series of documents looking at each of the potential scenarios for analysis. The scenarios were as follows:

- Keep all sites and look for cost reductions at each.
- Close all sites and develop a green-field operation.
- Close St. Helens and move all production to Crawley and Welwyn.
- Close Welwyn and move all production to Crawley and St. Helens.
- Close Crawley and move all production to St. Helens and Welwyn.
- Close St. Helens and Crawley and move all production to Welwyn.
- Close Welwyn and Crawley and move all production to St. Helens.
- Close Welwyn and St. Helens and move all production to Crawley.
- Close Welwyn and move production to Crawley.
- Close Crawley and move production to Welwyn.

Peter and I took these scenarios to a meeting with Albert Peters and the McKinsey consultant at Welwyn. During this discussion we narrowed down the options for full review. The focus in the discussion was on how to lever the volumes away from St. Helens. This seemed to be a key target, especially since SB had just announced the sale of the toiletries business, a significant part of production at St. Helens. I was charged with leading a subgroup to work on the options chosen for further review in more detail. The options I was given to look at were:

- Close all sites and move to a green-field site.
- Close St. Helens and move all production to Welwyn and Crawley.
- Close Welwyn and Crawley and move to a green-field site.
- Close Crawley and move production to Welwyn.

The option of closing Welwyn and moving production to Crawley had been removed from the agenda at that point because it was argued that disposal of the Crawley site to property developers would realize a much greater sum of money than disposal of the Welwyn site. The above list was agreed in the meeting and I left charged with my task.

The first part of the task was to project present volume requirements into the future and then work through each option with a team consisting of Brian Peterson (Production Manager, Welwyn); Harry Rogers (Engineering Manager, Welwyn); Alan Wall (Production Manager, Crawley); Lionel Platt (Engineering Manager, Crawley). We also had a representative from St. Helens at our first meeting, which was held at Welwyn.

Initially we started with the option of the two pharmaceutical plants (Crawley and Welwyn) absorbing the production from St. Helens. Then we considered the possibility that all might close and move to a green-field site. As we built operating models and derived financial cost configurations from them, we found that Welwyn cost significantly more to operate than the Beecham plants. Since I was close to the data I saw this pattern emerging first. In a meeting with Albert Peters, I raised my concern that in ignoring the potential closure of Welwyn and the subsequent transfer of production to Crawley, we could be missing an opportunity. He told me that he shared this view and felt that the options we had looked at so far would not produce the required cost reductions. He also pointed to the history of the old Beecham business. Basically, he could not see how the home of the original Beecham brand business at St. Helens could be sacrificed in the merger since previous attempts had failed. The chances of securing agreement to combine consumer and pharmaceutical production were low, even in the new organization. This really confirmed my intuition that there were other agendas in the meeting we had held at SB House.

I knew that this discussion had probably undermined the position that Peter Black had been building to defend the Welwyn site. In fact Welwyn closure had been off the work plan until this discussion. I felt terrible. By bringing it to the surface, rather than leaving it unsaid, I had probably given life to the idea. Worse still, on the night before the next steering group meeting, I had to meet the representatives from Welwyn to tell them that we were now to look at Welwyn closure. I was not comfortable with this because it contradicted the previous decision of the steering team. However, my concern that failure to evaluate the option would lead to a sub-optimal decision, led me to include it in our work plan for the following day. I asked Albert to call Peter Black to let him know that we would be looking at Welwyn closure the following day.

That evening I went to the Copthorne Hotel near the Crawley factory to meet up with Brian Peterson and Harry Rogers. I had to break the news to them that the following day we would be looking again at Welwyn closure. I did this in the bar at around 7:30p.m. as we got together for pre-dinner drinks. "Oh well, that's it then," said Brian Peterson, "I guess the bastards will shut us down now. Let's get drunk." My first concern was that the team should work well on the following day. So I asked him if he would still cooperate with me in conducting the review. He promised me that he would. He said that he intended to go down with dignity. So we got drunk and went to bed at around 4a.m.!

At the meeting on the following day, we reviewed the possibility of the Welwyn closure since this seemed to be the most financially viable case. The consumer group pulled out of the team in the following month on the basis that they were initiating their own manufacturing review. This left the recommendation from the UK team as the closure of the Welwyn factory, which duly happened.

Turning to the literature

The picture painted in the literature of how post-merger situations should be managed clearly did not match the experience of planning and factory rationalization I have been describing. The story I tell is one of groups of people trying to make sense of what was happening in an essentially messy, uncertain situation. We were a group of people trying to make sense of a situation characterized by the known and the unknown at the same time and trying to identify appropriate joint actions that would have very personal implications for a great many people. Our joint activity was not simply a rational, analytical process, although this did play a part. It was a process of communicative interaction, with aspects of power, politics and emotion. It was an activity of personal relating between individuals involving personal ambitions. Once again, the process was one of managers who were "in control" but "not in control" at the same time. One intention after another was emerging in our interaction, while the gesture of one was calling forth responses from another, at the same time.

The paradoxical nature of our activity is not easily made sense of from the perspective of mainstream thinking about management. Does this mean that our activity represents a management failure? I think not. Rather, it represents the inadequacy of mainstream thinking on mergers and acquisitions when it comes to making sense of what actually happens in these situations. It seems to me that most of the literature presents an idealization incapable of realization in practice. What is required is a perspective that encompasses the inevitably paradoxical nature of management activity.

My post-merger experience was one of participating in the social construction of new meaning, which emerged in legitimate, formal management processes, such as program and project management structures, and also at the same time in powerful, subtle and often conflicting processes of informal, shadow interaction. Furthermore, my experience of living through the merger illustrates the critical importance of the conversations all of us participated in. Most of these conversations were beyond the control of those outside our local interactions with each other and, indeed, beyond the control of any one of us. I suggest that the processes I am referring to are unpredictable and uncontrollable in the traditional management sense. For me, it is not that the post-merger activity at SB amounted to management failure at all, but rather, that mainstream prescriptions on mergers and acquisitions are idealistic aspirations that are impossible to carry out in the "real" world.

What this experience brought home to me was the extremely important part played by informal, personal relationships, emotion, power and politics in the joint sense making activities in which we were involved. Given this it would be fruitful to look at the literature on management networking.

Networking

A manager's network has been defined as a loosely organized social system consisting of informal cooperative relationships (Kaplan, 1984; Kotter, 1982; Mueller, 1986). It is suggested that such networks are formed "to assist managers in doing their jobs, carrying out their work agendas, and advancing their careers" (Michael and Yukl, 1993). The activities in which managers engage to develop and maintain networks are called networking behaviors (Burdett, 1991; Kilmann and Kilmann, 1991; Lipnack and Stamps, 1993) and the metaphor of streets and alleys is used to describe them:

> Effective managers are adept at working both the "streets" and the "alleys". The streets are the formal avenues by which work is accomplished – the formal chain of command and its written policies.

> The alleys are the informal avenues – the networks that enable
> managers to marshal the resources they need to get things done. . . .
> Networks sometimes appear to arise almost spontaneously.
>
> (Davis *et al.*, 1992: 234)

The prescriptions are for planned and managed networking behavior: "networks are carefully built based on criteria such as influence, skills, experience, position and so on" (Davis *et al.*, 1992: 234). Amongst the behavioral tips recommended are: develop a systematic approach to networking; analyze what you need and what you may be able to offer others; be sincerely interested in other people and their success because networks are based on mutual interest and genuine concern; get to know higher level managers in your group by volunteering as a resource for projects; draw a map of your potential network, including names and titles of both vertical and lateral employees.

Others suggest that success follows from being informed and that the information can be best gleaned "from contacts and sources in the broader business and wider community" (Burdett, 1991: 8). The energy required to sustain a network is identified as an important factor and this leads to suggestions that one should select those who have achieved "the highest level of professionalism . . . be patient, opportunistic and proactive in stalking the talented minority" (Burdett, 1991: 8). Furthermore, "it should not be presumed that networking becomes an activity that gets in the way of producing or delivering performance on the job. Successful executives integrate networking into their daily routine in a balanced and productive way" (Burdett, 1991: 9). Networking is said to work only where there is a "win-win" situation.

These approaches are somewhat mechanical and they present "hygienic" descriptions of behavior that does not resonate with my experience. They treat persons in a network as rational actors, as goal oriented utility maximizers who develop models of their networks (Burt, 1982; Marsden, 1982; Cook *et al.*, 1983), where access to information has a direct relationship to the size of the network (Burt, 1982). Concern with the qualities of relationship seems absent in this literature, which focuses more on network density and connectivity associated with ease of information exchange (Krackhardt, 1990). Density is defined as "the ratio of actual to potential ties among actors in a network; connectivity is the degree to which members of a network are linked together through direct or indirect ties" (Ibara, 1992: 170). Network analysts tend to use these terms (density and connectivity) to describe the development of both emergent and prescribed network structures. Networks can be analyzed in terms of their degrees of hierarchy and centralization: "A system is centralized to the extent that all relations in it involve a single actor. It has hierarchical structure to the extent that a single actor is the direct or indirect object of relations in it" (Burt, 1982: 61).

Others attempt to use network concepts to discuss a contrast between network and mechanistic or bureaucratic structures, which "comprised centralized, structured, single stranded, and sparse networks of asymmetric communication and control relations. In contrast, the organic organization associated with adaptive firms in turbulent environments was constituted by networks of dense, lateral, diffuse, and reciprocal relations" (Shrader et al., 1989: 45). Ibara (1992) argues that the action potential in an organization is "highly contingent on the degree of overlap or alignment between prescribed and emergent networks" (171). Weick (1979) explored the co-existence of prescribed and emergent networks and used the concept of coupling to describe the inter-relationship between the prescribed and emergent networks. A state of loose coupling entails highly disjointed formal and emergent structures with the task focuses of each possibly at cross-purposes. Orton and Weick (1990) suggest that organizations contain interdependent elements that vary in number and strength. They argue that loose and tight coupling exist simultaneously: "To state that an organization is a loosely coupled system is the beginning of a discussion not the end. What elements are loosely coupled? What domains are they coupled on? What are the characteristics of the couplings and decoupling?" (Orton and Weick, 1990: 219). Others concerned with the relationship characteristics of networks have looked at elements of power and the basis of control (Pfeffer and Salanick, 1978), and expressions of friendship and the exchange of liking and social support (Fombrun, 1982).

Thinking about networks in the ways described above suggests, for me, somewhat cold, mechanical, deliberate interactions with others motivated by desires to improve personal networks. However, my experience of the post-merger situation was of a messy process of relating, involving emotional conversations in which meaning arose. In this process my relationships evolved. I met Albert Peters when the merger occurred. The emergence of the action from the conversation that occurred had, for me, very little to do with the intentional setting up of a network. In fact I had not deliberately done this at all; yet the behavior described could be used to support a network view. Meaningful networks develop naturally and are alive in the conversations and experiences we have as we go about our work. The most effective networks for me have not been deliberately put together. Indeed, I have never done this deliberately and yet I continually converse with many different people on personal and business topics as I go about doing my job. The prescriptions provided by some in the literature seem hollow and meaningless, without the purpose and felt need that sustain attention and generate energy. My experience is of a number of persons engaging in conversations in a number of different locations in the living present as they go about their work. Each person is pursuing his or her own goals and yet they become intertwined as agendas emerge. Within the shifting relationships and power plays, old relationships or ties are weakened and new ones are formed. In my story of post-merger interaction, these shifts seemed to occur as our conversations led us to form new meanings and take actions that we might not have done, had we not conversed in the way that we did.

The emergent nature of the networks I experienced is closer to DiMaggio's (1992) description: "the population of engaged actors is not fixed (although the population of potential actors may be); actors improvise to create new relations or modify old ones; actors have more or less free access to one another; uncertainty is high; and actors have numerous objectives, or, . . . find goals poor guides to action" (122). DiMaggio suggests that the idea of a "practical-actor" rather than a rational actor seems to be more appropriate. I would go further and suggest a "pragmatic-actor" reflecting the manager's skill in handling the evolving flux of experience. This pragmatic-actor is able to sense the emergence of pattern of conversation and relationship and is able to use this sense of pattern to act effectively into it, accepting both the unpredictability and the capacity to influence what happens. What is important here is trust as a quality of relationship that emerges in conversational exchanges and facilitates them at the same time.

Conclusion

The merger represented a major transformation in the identities of two companies and their thousands of employees and shareholders, as well as for their competitors, suppliers, customers and regulatory authorities across many countries. As the first transatlantic merger in the history of the pharmaceutical industry, it could not have been a more significant change. However, there was not a change model in sight and how it all evolved cannot sensibly be ascribed to some plan formulated well in advance of what happened. Nor can it be ascribed to intentional networking activities. Indeed it would be hard to identify a beginning to this transformation because it emerged from such a long history. An arbitrary beginning might be the conversation between two men in a hotel room, in which they sought to make sense of a new potential future for their companies. On their own admission, the most sensitive theme in their early conversations related to who was going to be the CEO, surely a personal, emotional, power issue. The trust they developed as they talked and the conviction they built up that they could make it work became the major driving forces. These conversational exchanges were therefore critical in making sense of the potential opportunity and central to the actions that followed.

A central theme in the conversations between the two CEOs of the merging companies had to do with achieving outcomes they individually desired. Their "deal" emerged in conversations as they made sense of where they found themselves and tried to control their own futures. This "in control" image was then projected across the merging organizations as the two men sought to eradicate emotion and ensure that decisions were made on a factual basis. However, my story shows that far from achieving this, the imposed control simply sent feelings deeper underground. As relationships formed and re-formed in the shifting process of integration and rationalization, individuals and groups developed business cases based on their views of what was better or worse for them, as everybody sought to survive. The analytical tools they used in developing their business cases were often rhetorical devices or channels of energies and anxieties.

The harder the legitimate authorities tried to ensure that emotions were pushed aside, the more aware the targets of this control became of the issue and the more emotions surfaced. It was impossible to remove emotion. The structures used did help contain anxieties to some degree since they provided some tangible focal point through a tighter definition of the task at hand. The tension between the structured and unstructured surfaced in the conversations between those trying to make sense of their roles in the post-merger situation. An unspoken pattern of power relations seemed to spread across the merging organizations, perhaps as cascading responses to the power relations emerging in the conversations between the two CEOs. The initial forming phase of the UK factory integration team seemed to have some kind of unspoken patterning process from which emerged a pecking order, subsequently influencing decisions. The spontaneous formation of a discernible pattern had an important effect on behavior and yet it happened in a manner that was alongside the intended, legitimately applied control frameworks and often in spite of them.

The use of formal power in an attempt to create an environment that was more fluid both worked and did not work at the same time. By increasing the threat it forced people to be less trusting in general and to rely on their older, stronger relationships rather than build new alliances. This may have stifled some of the more creative thinking that was actually being sought. However, the adamant position taken by the new CEO regarding the required growth target for the business did seem to surface more opportunities but also caused a great deal of consternation. In a sense the combination of the formal power coupled with the use of the target seemed to cause some shifts in thinking and behavior. These outcomes were not predictable, though, with some groups digging in as they saw more threat in trying to achieve the target than sitting where they were.

It would seem that by maintaining the position he did, Bauman helped to create an environment that increased the potential for something to emerge. He and Wendt deliberately tried to remove the emotional dimension by getting people to focus on logical analysis. However, much more complex dynamics were at work, which were not controllable through the exercising of formal power. The outcomes depended upon the relationships that people developed, the sense they made of the situation they found themselves in, and the actions they took motivated as individuals to succeed in their lives.

For most of us, the merger created a sense of losing control over our lives, a threat to vitally important aspects of the quality of our lives, as levels of uncertainty rose significantly. Patterns that held important meaning and seemed so solid and reliable were disrupted overnight. This resulted in rising anxiety and increased searching for ways to regain control over what seemed to be key aspects of our lives. My experience of the merger of SKB and Beecham indicates that much evolved in the interpersonal interactions that took place during the merger process as each of us struggled to make our own meanings in the circumstances in which we found ourselves. It is my belief that no amount of planning could have reduced this "messiness," which seemed to be a necessary and natural part of developing a new sense of purpose and place with my new colleagues. The disruption and reconfiguration of relationships and informal power patterns I experienced in the merger process seemed to be self-organizing in nature and dependent on how people formed their relationships under high levels of uncertainty. From my perspective, the ability of those I interacted with to generate relationships, which were high on trust and seemed able to help contain anxiety, were useful and important to me. The literature gives a surface description of factors that may or may not be relevant and provides little indication of what is really going on in the highly ambiguous and uncertain merger situation. Effective managers are thought to be those who refuse to allow political behavior to emerge. However, this behavior inevitably does emerge and it is an important element of the self-organizing processes I experienced.

There were no comprehensive plans from above according to which the integration process proceeded. What was striking was the rather minimal prescriptions from higher up the hierarchy: the statement that the new company was to be an integrated healthcare business, the setting of a global profit target, the call for integrating and rationalizing production facilities to reduce costs. All of these pronouncements or intentions seem to have emerged in the local discussion between top executives and amounted to gestures made to the rest of the organization. There were gestures made by the new Chairman and CEO, which called forth all manner of responses from others throughout the organization that those gesturing could not have foreseen. It was up to people in many different parts of the organization to respond in a meaningful way and we did not immediately know what a meaningful response would be. Hence the many conversations that took place, in which we sought to create new meanings. The responses were processes of negotiation in local situations in the living present in which analytical tools were used as persuasive devices in a process of communicative interaction in which new patterns of meaning emerged. So, there were plans and projections but they constituted tools used by people in communicative interaction taking the form of political processes in the living present of local situations. There was the local situation of the two men at the top and there were many, many other local situations throughout the organization. The evolving identity of the integrating companies emerged in the interaction between all of these local situations. An important aspect of this process had to do with how people dealt with the anxieties generated by the uncertainties of the merger. The paradox of control was evident in the fact that the situation was both known and unknown at the same time and people were taking intentional actions as well as responding to the gestures of others at the same time.

Mainstream ways of thinking about the nature of management do not assist me to make sense of the kinds of messy, paradoxical situations I have described. In the next chapter I turn to a perspective that places paradox at the center of the explanation.

5 Making sense of the paradox of control in merger situations

The account given in the last two chapters of the merger and its aftermath is essentially about how the particular organization in which I was working came to be what it was, and in an important sense how I and others came to be what we were. In other words, the stories had to do with the evolution of a particular organization's identity and, therefore, its difference from other organizations. But it was not just some abstract entity that was evolving. It was human persons, the people who constituted the organization, who evolved collectively and individually. Those stories were about the pattern of a particular organization's movement into the future, its strategic direction, and the causes of that pattern of movement. At the same time those stories were about the pattern of movement into the future of human persons, including me.

In relation to those stories, I pointed to how the literature on organizations and their management indicates particular ways of making sense of that movement and I dealt with some of the assumptions upon which those particular ways of making sense are built. It is usually implicitly assumed that effective organizations are moving toward a known future state, one that is already given in some way, in order to achieve some optimal arrangement and so realize chosen goals. It is assumed that effective movement can be more or less regular and that effective organizations are more or less stable. If one focuses attention on organizations in this way, it is not at all problematic to propose that managers are "in control" of an organization's movement into the future, that their choices are the cause of the organization's movement, and that competent managers design their organization's future in advance of realizing it. When we find that we cannot stay "in control" in this sense, then the only explanation seems to be our own ignorance and incompetence. And in focusing attention on "the organization" in this instrumental way, we easily lose sight of the fact that an organization's identity is the collective and individual identities of human persons.

I have also been expressing the view that it is difficult, and deeply unfulfilling, to try to make sense of my pre- and post-merger experience using explanatory frameworks built on these assumptions. My experience, as reflected in the stories, suggests that my organization was moving toward a future that was unknown in very important respects at the time. Indeed, that we as people were moving toward personal futures which were also unknown to us at the time. Looking back on the experience, it seems to me that I was participating with other managers across the organization in a process in which our own and our organization's future was under perpetual construction by us in interaction with people in other organizations. It was what groups of us were doing together in many different places across this global organization that was constructing the future. And what we were perpetually constructing together was nothing less than the identity of our organization and in important ways, our own identities. It was our actions, up and down the hierarchy, and across the geographic spread of the organization, which were sustaining and transforming the identity of our organization and, thus, its difference from others. In other words, the movement of our organization was fundamentally paradoxical in that it both sustained its identity (the known, sameness, continuity) and, at the same time, transformed it (the unknown, difference, discontinuity).

In this chapter, I want to point to a way of making sense of my experience that places the kind of paradox I have just referred to at the center of the explanation, namely, a perspective from which organizations are understood as complex responsive processes of relating. This perspective has itself emerged in ongoing conversations, in many of which I participated as a member of a doctoral group at the Complexity and Management Centre of the University of Hertfordshire. This perspective has been articulated in some detail, and compared with other perspectives, in the first two volumes (Stacey, Griffin and Shaw, 2000; Stacey, 2001) in this series. In this chapter, I present a summary of the complex responsive process perspective (drawn from Stacey, 2001), and link it back to the stories of the last two chapters. In chapters six and seven I continue with an account of my experience at SB, indicating in further detail how I might make sense of it from the complex responsive process perspective.

Organizations as complex responsive processes of relating

The stories told in the last two chapters are all about the continuity and transformation of the organization in which I worked for many years. I reflected on the way in which the identity of SK&F was transformed by the development of Tagamet. It was still felt to be SK&F by those who had worked for it for many years but at the same time it was a very different SK&F. I talked about the transformation in which SK&F became SKB. The organization was quite different in many ways after the acquisition of Beckman, but it still felt like SK&F to me and, I sense, to many others. The history of SK&F, and that of Beckman too, was still relevant to any understanding of what SKB was. I explored in some detail a few of the stories around the transformation of SKB into SB. The latter was certainly very different to the former and yet there was also, at the same time, continuity. Over the decades, as its identity transformed in ways no one could have foreseen, it continued to be a complex process of joint action in which growing thousands of people cooperated in the development and production of pharmaceutical products. Many of those products were novel in ways that no one foresaw well in advance of their development. These complex processes of joint, cooperative action encompassed the daily production of known products such as Contac and the development of new ones such as Tagamet, as well as the regular procedures of budgeting and the major discontinuities of mergers and factory rationalization. All of these cooperative activities, however, were made possible by the ongoing communication between the people who were the organization. The joint action of producing and developing products, of budgeting, merging and rationalizing, all arose in the communicative interaction between the people who were the organization, whether at the top in the CEO's office or much lower at the factory in Welwyn. From the production of Contac, to the negotiation of the merger, to the rationalization of the UK factories, the stories had one common feature, namely, people talking to each other. Cooperative joint action of all kinds was made possible by the ongoing processes of communicative interacting, by the continuous process of people relating to each other.

It is these processes of ordinary, everyday communicative interaction that constitute complex responsive processes of relating. The process of perpetual construction of an organization's future, as the continuity and transformation of its identity, is one of communicative interaction, in the living present, between humans and the context they find themselves in.

In other words the cause of the movement toward an organization's known–unknown future lies in the detailed, self-organizing process of bodily communicative interaction as it forms and is formed by itself at the same time. This circular, reflexive, self-referential causality forms and is formed by human interaction. Intention and design are all seen as aspects of these complex responsive processes of relating, but only aspects in much wider, far more complex processes of human relating. In their communicating and relating, members of the organization did prepare plans and they did undertake rational, quantitative analyses of proposed actions. But these cannot be equated with decision making, nor can they be said to have caused the evolution of the organization. They were simply tools, sometimes very important tools, in wider processes of communicative interaction.

Crucially, these wider processes of communicative relating were essentially to do with power. In our communicative interaction and our power relating, primarily expressed in endless conversations with each other, we negotiated our daily going on with each other and what emerged was the pattern of evolution, the identity, of our organization. The identities of our organization and of ourselves were creatively transformed in the following sense:

> Creative, in this context, has the sense not of original creativity as performed by the genius but of living spontaneously, in action and reaction, with the contents of one's cultural life . . . One need not be what is called a creative artist or scientist or statesman, but one must be able to participate meaningfully in their original creations. Such participation is creative insofar as it changes that in which one participates, even if in very small ways . . . Everyone who lives creatively in meanings affirms himself as a participant in these meanings. He affirms himself as receiving and transforming reality creatively.
>
> (Tillich, 1952: 46)

The complex responsive process perspective immediately focuses attention on how problematic it is to suppose that managers are "in control" of their organization's movement into the future. The choices of effective managers are not simply the cause of an organization's movement into the future; rather, they simultaneously form and are formed by that movement. Choices emerge in the movement at the same time as they shape it. Competent managers design tools, which they use in the communicative interaction that constructs their organization's future, without knowing in advance what that future will be. From this perspective, it comes as no surprise that we cannot stay "in control" of our organization and instead of ascribing this to ignorance and incompetence, we focus attention on the creative nature of our participation in which we change what we participate in, "even if in very small ways." And in focusing attention on "the organization" in this way, we cannot lose sight of the fact that an organization's evolving identity is the evolving collective and individual identities of human persons.

The central focus on management as participation in the making of meaning immediately focuses attention on another important matter. The loss of meaning experienced in times of major discontinuous change engenders anxiety and with it comes feelings of helplessness: "Helplessness in the state of anxiety can be observed in animals and humans alike. It expresses itself in loss of direction, inadequate reactions" (Tillich, 1952: 36–7). When we are in this state we seek to defend ourselves in many different ways, and at least some of these ways may actually make it more difficult to restore meaning. Instead of immediately judging what we do as incompetent, therefore, the complex responsive process perspective encourages us to understand what we are doing in terms of defenses against anxiety and attempts to restore meaning. It is then quite understandable that in the aftermath of the merger, a group of us simply carried on making plans as before, almost as if nothing had happened. It becomes quite clear why exhortations to eschew personal ambition and emotion in working on the factory rationalization project could not be complied with. We also begin to see the interactions from which rationalization plans emerged as a creative process of constructing meaning.

This perspective leads to a reappraisal of what it means to manage effectively. Instead of defining effective managers in terms of rational analysts who put emotion and the struggle for personal survival to one side, we come to understand effective management as the quality of courage to carry on participating in the creation of personal and collective meaning, if only in small ways, in spite of the anxiety and helplessness engendered by the loss of direction.

The above paragraphs provide a brief overview of some of the most important elements of the complex responsive process perspective. In the following sections, I briefly elaborate further on key aspects, namely:

- Local interaction in the living present.
- The use of plans, procedures and systems as tools of communicative interaction.

- The wider processes of communicative interaction.
- Power relations.
- The thematic patterning of communicative interaction.
- The conversational life of the organization.

Having explored these points I will return to the implications for control.

Local interaction in the living present

From the complex responsive process perspective, sense is made of organizational life by attending to the ordinary, everyday communicative interacting between people at their own local level of interaction in the living present. The local nature of interaction is clear in the story about the production of Contac in chapter two. The quality of the product depended upon the communicative interaction, in the living present of each day, of those working together in a particular place. But the point also applies to managers and leaders at the top of the organizational hierarchy, for example, the chief executive. Although the chief executive acts in relation to the whole of an organization, he or she talks most frequently about matters of greatest concern to a relatively small group of trusted others, that is, in the living present of a local situation. The chief executive's important communicative interactions take place, therefore, in the local situation of other senior executives. In chapter three, I reported Bob Bauman's description of the conversations he had with Henry Wendt in the living present of a hotel room and how these conversations were part of a process in which the future of both SKB and Beecham were being constructed.

Of course, what came out of the communicative interaction in that hotel room had a much bigger impact across the organization than the communicative interaction in the Contac production area did, but the process was the same. People were in conversation with each other, in the living present of their local situation, and it was in this communicative interaction that other forms of joint action emerged. In each case, communicative interaction was an ongoing process of one gesturing to another, calling forth responses from the other. When a chief executive makes a public gesture, it potentially calls forth responses in much larger numbers of others than is the case with the less powerful. However, the makers of the gestures cannot determine what those responses will be, whether they are chief executives or production workers. Bauman and Wendt called on all of us to set aside personal ambition and emotion in order to make purely rational decisions. Our response was to proceed in a different way and I imagine that we were not the only ones in the corporation to do so. To ask people in a highly charged, anxiety provoking situation to set aside emotion and concerns of personal survival is highly unlikely to call forth a conforming response. But just what responses it will call forth are unlikely to be predictable, as the story of the factory rationalization in the previous chapter shows. No one can determine the dynamic of interaction within an organization because that dynamic depends upon what others, both within that organization and in other organizations, are doing. In other words, an individual, or a group of individuals, powerful or otherwise, can make gestures of great importance but the responses called forth will emerge in local situations in the living present where an organization's future is perpetually being constructed.

Clearly, powerful managers often have major, widespread effects on the "whole" organization but these effects emerge in their local communicative interaction and call forth responses in many other local situations, all in the living present. It is in these interactions of continuous gesture and response that the future of the organization is constructed as the continuity and transformation of its identity. So, in their local conversations, Bauman and Wendt determined who would be chief executive and in doing so made a gesture to all in the organization. This was followed by other gestures such as the statement about an integrated healthcare business and the call for the merging companies to be integrated in a rational manner. The responses in one local situation, the one I participated in, were varied and in that local communicative interaction a plan emerged for factory rationalization. The focus of attention, in trying to make sense of what happens, shifts from the chief executive's statement, seen as a communicative tool, to the processes in which the statement or tool arises and to the widespread local situations in which they have their effects. Instead of taking it for granted that powerful chief executives actually individually change organizations directly through their intended actions, the complex responsive process perspective invites one to explore the communicative processes in which the images and the fantasies about leaders, as well as their mere presence, all affect local processes of communicative interaction in the living present.

How is this view of local interactions across a global enterprise compatible with the recognizable coherence of that global enterprise? In other words, how is it possible for thousands of people interacting in their local situations to produce global order, in the absence of a global program or blueprint? The answer has to do with the intrinsic self-organizing/emergent properties of interaction itself. Work in the complexity sciences demonstrates the possibility that interactions between large numbers of entities, each responding to others on the basis of its own local organizing principles, will produce coherent patterns with the potential for novelty in certain conditions, namely, the paradoxical dynamics at the "edge of chaos." In other words, the very process of self-organizing interaction, when richly connected enough, has the inherent capacity to spontaneously produce coherent pattern in itself, without any blueprint or program. Furthermore, when the interacting entities are different enough from each other, that capacity is one of spontaneously producing novel patterns in itself. In other words, abstract systems can pattern themselves where those patterns have the paradoxical feature of continuity and novelty, identity and difference, at the same time. By analogy, the ongoing process of communicative interaction, the endless gesturing and responding between people who are different from each other, may be thought of as self-organizing relating, having intrinsic patterning capacity. This is what is meant by complex responsive process of relating and it amounts to thinking in terms of a particular causal framework where the process is one of perpetual construction of the future as both continuity and potential transformation at the same time. I think this describes what happened when a small group of very different people, some from SKB and some from Beecham, came together and began to talk about how we might rationalize the factories. There was no plan or program worth the name. We really were operating in the unknown and experiencing the anxiety this brings. But in the living present of that local situation we interacted in a way that produced new meaning from which the chosen rationalization option emerged.

The tools of communicative interaction

Communicative interaction between people in organizations involves the use of highly sophisticated tools: telephones, e-mail, documents of all kinds, systems of information and control, statements of visions, missions, values, policies and so on. When people interact with each other in the living present of their local situations, they communicate in ways that use all of these tools.

The story of the factory rationalization following the announcement of the merger, for example, was clearly a process of communicative action involving a small number of people. One of the tools we used was a rational, quantitative analysis of the costs and benefits of different options for closure and relocation. However, that analysis was not a straightforward calculation that produced a decision. I hope I have made it clear how it was a tool used in a negotiating process to direct attention and persuade. The rationalization decisions themselves emerged in the communicative interaction between us and that interaction was patterned in an emergent way by many themes forming, while being formed by, our conversations with each other. These conversations referred to documents setting out abstract-systematic frameworks of cash flow analyses and risk factor appraisals. We used these documents as rhetorical tools to persuade each other in processes of negotiating with, and accounting to each other for the positions we took. All of these tools are aspects of the process of institutionalization and the constraints it imposes on action. It is necessary to produce them and negotiate their meaning as part of the process of accounting for choices made to higher levels of the management hierarchy. It was only possible to participate in discussions around post-merger developments by talking in the prescribed language of cash flows, risk factor analyses, budget constraints and approval procedures. The tools shape themes in the wider process of communicative interaction, both enabling and exercising powerful constraints on that communication.

However, the particular language of tools can create a kind of myopia in which we no longer "see" other aspects of the wider process of communicative interaction we are participating in. In other words, it is important not to mistake the tools for communicative interaction itself because this leads to obscuring the nature of the themes patterning the decision-making process, creating the illusion that the decision is largely a calculation. This then acts as a defense against noticing the underlying power relations and the ideological positions sustaining or shifting those power relations. Mistaking the tools for the process of communicative interaction also obscures an understanding of the anxiety provoked by the potential for transformation and the resulting unconscious themes patterning the experience.

The wider processes of communicative interaction

When one equates the institutionalized tools of communicative interaction with the wider process, one focuses attention on the formal, conscious, legitimate processes of relating. However, it is well known that no organization can function without informal relationships as well. Certainly, my experience of participating in the rationalization process bears this out. I was invited to participate in the first place because of my personal relationship with Peter Black and as the group developed its work I came to form an informal relationship with others that had a bearing on how that work evolved. The formal and the informal are inseparable aspects of processes of communicative interaction, and many of the themes patterning communicative interaction are unconscious, often linked to others protecting them from exposure to consciousness. In the last chapter, I described how the rationalization group unconsciously established a pecking order within minutes of our first meeting and how that pecking order continued to influence the work of the group.

Furthermore, communicative interaction may be patterned by themes that are not strictly speaking legitimate. In this context, legitimate means communicative interactions that can be openly conducted, in public as it were. But there are also themes that are neither illegitimate nor illegal but are nevertheless felt, either consciously or unconsciously, inappropriate to express openly in public. These have been called shadow themes (Stacey, 2000), for example, those taking the form of gossip (Elias and Scotson, 1994), or humor, parody and mockery (Bakhtin, 1986), usually only freely expressed in small trusted groups. In the story of the rationalization program I tried to convey the sense of small groups of us talking to each other at the bar, raising important issues there before they could be more publicly voiced, for example to do with reinstating the Welwyn factory on the possible closure list.

Themes, with all their multiple aspects of formal–informal, conscious–unconscious, legitimate–shadow, are continuously reproducing and potentially transforming themselves in the process of interaction itself. Running throughout this ongoing self-organizing communication there is the phenomenon of power.

Power relations

To go on together, people have to account to each other for what they do. In other words, the maintenance of relationships imposes constraint. Power is a constraint that excludes some communicative actions and includes others. However, at the same time, power enables. As they take and make turns in communication with each other, people both enable and constrain each other at the same time. Communicative interaction, therefore, immediately establishes power differences in which some people are "in" and others are "out." The very process of turn taking/turn making, which is the central process of conversation, makes the dynamic of inclusion and exclusion an inevitable and irremovable property of human communicative interaction, quite simply because when one person takes a turn, others are at that moment excluded from doing so. This inevitable dynamic has very important consequences. If communicative interaction is essential, not only for the survival of every individual, but also for the continued reproduction and transformation of their very selves, or identities, then any exclusion must be felt as very threatening.

So, despite their best efforts, Bauman and Wendt sent a signal to the new organization through the way that their agreement had turned out. When Bauman took over the reins of the new company, it generated a theme that organized experience in many local situations. The theme was one in which we all felt that former Beecham people somehow had the upper hand and this triggered responding themes. Peter Black had been the leading SKB production person in the UK for at least five years and he was not going to just lie down and get walked over by these Beecham people. Realizing that the approach would be process driven the major power play would be via the McKinsey consultants. If they endorsed the approach being advocated then there was a chance that the process could bias the outcome. It seemed that it was impossible to remove personal bias from the process.

The process of communicative interaction reproduces and transforms themes of emergent patterns of collaboration, and at the same time reproduces and transforms themes to do with inclusion and exclusion, or power, and these arouse feelings of anxiety, which trigger themes to deal with that anxiety in some way. The themes triggered by anxiety may well have to do with re-patterning the dynamic of inclusion and exclusion, with shifting the relations of power. These and other themes triggered by anxiety may well disrupt collaboration and they may also be highly destructive. However, without such disruptions to current patterns of collaboration and power relations there could be no emergent novelty in communicative interaction and hence no novelty in any form of human action. The reason for saying this is that disruptions generate diversity. One of the central insights of the complexity sciences is how the spontaneous emergence of novelty depends upon diversity (Allen, 1998).

Furthermore, there is a link between anxiety and the use of fantasy to cope with it. The result can be misunderstanding to varying degrees, even serious breakdown in the whole process of communicative interaction. Again, however, there is a close relationship between fantasy and misunderstanding, on the one hand, and the emergence of novelty, on the other. Fantasy is close to imaginative elaboration and misunderstanding triggers a search for understanding thereby provoking continued imaginative elaboration and communication. It is in such continued struggles for meaning, and the imaginative elaboration going with it, that the novel emerges.

In the merger situation, people seen as powerful because of the self-confidence they displayed and the connections they were known to have, were able to exert some kind of controlling influence over others. It seemed that their self-confidence provided a solid sense of presence, allowing others to feel that this person had a way of handling the anxiety of the uncertain situation. This kind of power arises as a feeling in interaction between people, almost in spite of their intentions. It seems to be an elusive property achieved through some form of connectedness between people, created transiently in relationships. Perhaps, in a sense, it is an illusion, an invention of our projections onto others that "they know," that they have "sussed out the right answer" and that we are wrong, or somehow less advantaged than they. In a sense, these powerful people might become containers for others' anxieties about the future. Somehow we vest capabilities in these people to control the uncertainties that cause us to feel concern in our lives. Yet, as we have seen in the merger situation, everyone concerned was experiencing the same kind of uncertainties. Credibility required demonstrating delivery, even under the most adverse and unimaginable circumstances.

As the merger began to disrupt the formal hierarchy, previous patterns of relationships began to dissolve, leaving only the most solid relationships in place, based on deep levels of trust. In a sense, the position taken by Bauman about removing emotion was driving those who were trying to look after themselves deeper and deeper underground – but not away, and definitely not towards analytical decision making. Ironically, this would mean that those who wanted to protect their previous positions would collude, thereby undermining the outcome desired by those introducing the heavy controls in the first place. Financial analysis, discounted cash-flow assessments of investments or of significant business decisions, requires selective choice of data to be made for inclusion in the financial models. The weight attributed to elements of the data and the risks involved relies on intuitive processes that themselves rely on choices that can clearly be influenced by emotional attachments to certain outcomes possibly giving preference to one over any of the others. New relationships were built up – such as the one between Albert Peters and myself. It was only as we explored each other's motives that he began to see I was determined to find some kind of right answer from a purist viewpoint. My container for the anxieties related to the task was my felt detachment from the manufacturing organization and my wish to leave. I believed that if I did this task well it would set me up to move elsewhere and so I did things that I could not have contemplated if I was staying. He had his motives too – he wanted his site to become the best and most important in SmithKline Beecham and with it his importance would increase.

My sense that perhaps Albert knew that the answer we were going to produce was somehow not as good as it could be motivated my question to him when I went to Crawley. This really confirmed my intuition that there were other agendas in the meeting we had held at SB House. Yet the answer could have been anything we wanted it to be. The emphasis placed on certain elements in the discounted cash-flow analyses that we did to examine the return on the different options were critically dependent upon where we intuitively placed assumptions around capital expenditure, ongoing running costs and so on. The business cases, though rationally argued, were based on foundations of what made most sense to us and what we felt we could sell to the merger management committee. Although Bauman had set targets, he did not have any superior knowledge to know what the right answer should be either. The initial goals for the new company had been based on what was felt to be necessary to justify the merger to the key shareholders, not a number built bottom up. The action of resurrecting the possibility of closing Welwyn came from a feeling that there was a better answer somewhere than the one we were looking at. This feeling emerged in a "behind closed doors" conversation as part of a sharing of some thoughts and fears about the process we were going through. My discomfort with the way things were going precipitated the conversation with Albert that moved us to act together, but I am sure now for different motives.

Power relations are sustained by ideology. A key aspect of ideology is the binary oppositions that characterize it and the most basic of these is the distinction between "them" and "us." Ideology is thus a form of communication that preserves the current order by making that current order seem natural. In this way, ideological themes organize the communicative interactions of individuals and groups. It is a patterning process, that is, narrative themes of inclusion and exclusion organizing themselves in perpetual reproduction and potential transformation. Ideology exists only in the speaking and acting of it. Ideology emerges in a self-organizing process of gossip. Streams of gossip stigmatize and blame the outsider group while similar streams of gossip praise the insider group. Such gossip and other ways of talking attribute "charisma" to the powerful and "stigma" to the weak, so reinforcing power differences.

Bauman disrupted set patterns, reflecting an ideology of control, through his absolute requirement that the growth target must be met. This was based on his perception that it was a survival issue for the new company in the eyes of its shareholders and therefore for him personally in his position, to hit the growth target. The attachment to 15 percent at all costs led him to use his positional power in a somewhat dictatorial fashion to force other managers to conform to his view of the situation by accepting his requirements.

The conversational life of an organization

From the complex responsive process perspective, the future of an organization is perpetually constructed in the conversational exchanges of its members as they carry out their tasks (see Boje, 1991, 1995; Weick, 1995). How do these conversations pattern, while being patterned by, communication? An answer is suggested by analogies from the complexity sciences, namely, the dynamics of the stable, the unstable and the "edge of chaos."

Some conversational processes display the dynamics of stability when patterned by habitual, highly repetitive themes. In this dynamic, people are "stuck" and their conversation loses the potential for transformation. Identity arising in "stuck" conversation is continuity with little variation. The quality is lifeless, depressing, even obsessive and compulsive. Other conversational processes display the dynamics of instability in which coherent pattern is lost as fragments of conversation trigger other fragments with little thematic structure. One might characterize such conversation as disintegrative. The quality is confusion and distress with a fragmenting of identity. Yet other conversational processes display the dynamic analogous to the "edge of chaos," where patterning themes have the paradoxical characteristics of continuity and spontaneity at the same time. The felt qualities of such conversations are liveliness, fluidity and energy but also a feeling of grasping at meaning and coherence. There is excitement but also, at the same time, tension and anxiety. When conversational processes are characterized by this kind of dynamic, they have the potential for transformation. A further analogy from the complexity sciences demonstrates the possibility that it is only interaction between diverse entities that gives rise to the potential for transformation. With regard to human conversation, this analogy suggests that transformative potential arises in conversations when participants are diverse, that is, sufficiently different to each other. In these conditions interaction may amplify small differences into major discontinuous changes in understanding. It is well known that cross-discipline and cross-functional conversations stimulate new insights. It is in their struggling to understand each other in fluid, spontaneous conversational exchanges that people create new knowledge.

However, this is by no means an easy communicative process. It entails misunderstanding, which is usually experienced as frustrating, even distressing, as well as stimulating and exciting. Furthermore, the pressure to relieve the frustration may well lead to the closing down of conversational exploration. Conversational processes having transformative potential, by their very nature threaten the continuity of identity. If a group of people have spent the past decades thinking and talking in a particular way, for example, in terms of being "in control," their individual and collective identities are inevitably closely tied up with that way of thinking and talking. Conversations that challenge it hold out the potential for transformation but at the same time they threaten identity. In other words, conversations with transformative potential inevitably arouse anxiety at a deep existential level.

Conversations with transformative potential inevitably threaten current power relations, which are also an important aspect of organizational identity. As issues emerge in an evolving organization, people find themselves clustering around particular issues. Some of these clusters will interact communicatively in ways patterned by themes forming unofficial ideologies, which may threaten the official ideology. The sensed undermining of existing power relations provokes reactions that once again seek to shut down exploratory conversation with their transformative, knowledge creating potential. Conversations that threaten current power relations raise the real fear of exclusion and so also prompt moves to shut them down.

The conversational life of an organization is potentially transformative when through the diversity of participation it has the dynamics of fluid spontaneity, liveliness and excitement, inevitably accompanied by misunderstanding, anxiety provoking threats to identity and challenges to official ideology and current power relations.

Conclusion

When one understands organizations as complex responsive processes of relating, it becomes clear that managers cannot be "in control" in any simple way. However, this does not mean that managers are "not in control." Rather, managers are "in control" and "not in control" at the same time. In this paradoxical process, the key management attribute is the courage to carry on participating creatively in the conversation in which new meaning emerges, in spite of not knowing. This requires an ability to live with the anxiety of paradox and calls for an understanding of organizational life that focuses attention on the qualities and patterns of relating in local situations in the living present.

6 Measuring performance is not quite as simple as it seems

- Why measure performance?
- Project Dashboard
- Was performance measurement really the task?
- Ideology and power

In the last chapter, I briefly summarized a complex responsive process perspective on organizations. This perspective resonates with my experience, from which I conclude that attempts to understand organizations from a macro perspective meet with limited success. The complex responsive process perspective suggests paying much more attention to the micro detail of communicative interaction in local situations in the living present. This was the way my thinking was moving as I participated in the exercise to measure performance which I will describe in this chapter. Paying attention in this way helped me, I think, to be more effective, precisely because I was paying serious attention to aspects of what was going on in the conversations I engaged in, which previously I had tended to ignore.

Towards the end of 1995, I was appointed to a team called Project Dashboard, charged with putting together a set of performance measures for the leadership team of the Worldwide Supply Organization (WSO). The purpose of the performance measures was to indicate where WSO was and where it was going. At the first meeting of the project team, it was made very clear to us that our brief was confined to defining the most appropriate measures for the new organization and proposing a mechanism to put them in place. We were directed to produce a balanced approach that would bring both financial and operational measures together, so paving the way for a potential Economic Value Added (EVA) management approach to be brought in by 2000.

The approach we took was in line with the "SB Way" (a common approach introduced to manage the company on a day-to-day basis) in that one of the SB core management concepts was management by facts and data with measures being key to providing feedback. The CEO of the company used to say, "If you're not keeping score you're only practicing." In trying to operationalize this, we developed a list of what we thought were relevant measures and then held discussions with some of the site leaders and leadership team members to check on their validity. Before I recount my experience of this project I want to look briefly at the thinking underlying performance measurement.

Why measure performance?

The very name, "Project Dashboard" points to the kind of thinking underlying the call for performance measurement. The assumption is that successful performance depends upon first defining what successful outcomes would be, then identifying the key actions required to produce those outcomes, then measuring and monitoring the outcomes of actions actually undertaken and finally taking corrective action to stay on the path toward the pre-defined successful outcomes. The belief is that predictable business performance is achieved through targeting improvement activities at key performance indicators. Managers can then sleep more soundly knowing that key indicators are going in the right direction, even if they do not always know why. The trick is to find the right indicator to measure. Getting it right and staying in control is the aim.

What has been the outcome of this way of thinking in business as a whole?

> Most managers have known for years that their performance measurement systems track the wrong things. Financial indicators show where the company has been. They don't tell you until it is too late about key changes in, for example, customers, markets or technology.
>
> (Geanuracos and Meiklejohn, 1994: 2)

For the Total Quality Management (TQM) movement of the 1980s, the reason for measurement was to identify variations from pre-determined paths, and then to "detect assignable causes of variation in order to provide surveillance and feedback control" (Box *et al.*, 1978: 556). The TQM movement extended negative feedback control logic, previously applied to production and engineering activities, to management in general. Deming's philosophy was born of one key theme "If quality improvement could be reduced to one thought it would be to reduce variation" (Collins and Huge, 1993: 1). It was thought that this concept of quality was being applied in Japan to business management in general and the proposal was to extend it to Western companies. The same kind of principle was evident in the process management thinking of the early 1990s. If the process could be mapped out and wasteful elements removed, then it could be brought more under control. One of the keys to business re-engineering success was to measure the "right" things and bring them under control with the goal of achieving favorable final results.

The balanced scorecard

Research by Kaplan and Norton (1992, 1993, 1996) re-invigorated the measurement debate. They concluded that what you measure is what you get and went on to advocate the use of a balanced set of measures, which "includes financial measures that tell the results of actions already taken. And it complements the financial measures with operational measures on customer satisfaction, internal processes and the organization's innovation and improvement activities – operational measures that are the drivers of future financial performance" (Kaplan and Norton, 1992: 71). The purpose of the balanced scorecard was very definitely not control. On the contrary,

> The scorecard puts strategy and vision, not control, at the center. It establishes goals but assumes that people will adopt whatever behaviors and take whatever actions are necessary to arrive at these goals . . . Senior management may well know what the end result should be, but they cannot tell employees exactly how to achieve the result, if only because the conditions in which employees operate are constantly changing.
>
> (Kaplan and Norton, 1992: 79)

Kaplan and Norton (1992) suggested that each organization was unique and so should follow its own path in building a balanced scorecard. However, they did propose a generalized approach for organizations that had not yet defined their strategy and recommended a "systematic development plan to create a balanced scorecard and encourage commitment to the scorecard among senior and mid-level managers" (Kaplan and Norton, 1993: 138). The recommendation was that an organization should build a balanced scorecard through a systematic process that "builds consensus and clarity about how to translate a unit's mission and strategy into operational objectives and measures" (Kaplan and Norton, 1996: 294). The authors were keen to provide a process, which ensured that the scorecard represented the collective wisdom and energies of the senior executive team of the business unit. The process was also designed to support management teams who desired the scorecard to be an integral part of an organization's management process. They cited two instances where "an excellent scorecard was developed by very senior staff executives without actively engaging their senior management teams in the process" (Kaplan and Norton, 1996: 294) resulting in no change in the businesses. To deal with this type of failure, they advocated an implementation approach as follows:

1 Define the measurement architecture. This involves choosing a part of the business that operates as a stand-alone entity with its own innovations, operations, marketing, selling and service. This business unit would have its own customers, distribution channels and production operations. A test question is whether "the proposed organization has a strategy to accomplish its mission" (301). Typically, either an internal or an external architect should be appointed at this point.

2 Conduct interviews to identify strategic business units and corporate linkages so as not to "develop objectives and measures that optimize the SBU (strategic business unit) at the expense of other SBUs" (302).

3 Build consensus around strategic objectives. This is achieved by circulating draft material on the scorecard, the mission and the vision of the SBU to the top six to twelve executives and then conducting ninety-minute interviews with them. These interviews are conducted for two reasons. First, "to obtain their input on the company's strategic objectives and tentative proposals for balanced scorecard measures" (303). Second, to begin "the process of having top management think about translating strategy and objectives into tangible, operational measures, learning about the concerns that key individuals may have about developing and implementing the scorecard, and identifying potential conflicts among key participants" (303).

4 Executive workshop – first round. This is designed to deal with a synthesis of the issues raised in the interviews and to arrive at a shared view of the strategy. Voting is carried out to rank the objectives for the organization in the light of the strategy selected. This leads into the development by subgroups of the relevant measures to be set up.

5 Executive workshop – second round. This now broadens the scope of those involved to the executive team (6–12) plus their direct subordinates and a number of middle managers. Executives present the objectives and measurement proposals to subgroups that comment

on the measures and develop an implementation plan. The outputs are expected to be "a brochure to communicate the scorecard intentions and contents to all employees . . . [and] to encourage participants to formulate stretch objectives for each of the proposed measures, including targeted rates of improvement" (307).

6 Executive workshop – third round. This meeting now looks at a proposed implementation plan and consists of the senior executives only. It is carried out to "agree on an implementation program to communicate the scorecard to employees, integrate the scorecard into a management philosophy, and develop an information system to support the scorecard" (308).

Having encouraged potential users to follow this approach, Kaplan and Norton then recommend that management "begin using the scorecard within 60 days. Obviously a phase-in plan must be developed, but the 'best available' information should be used to focus the management agenda" (308).

"Economic Value Added"

Joel Stern and Bennett Stewart published their work on Economic Value Added (EVA) in 1990. This work attempted to show senior managers how the financial markets evaluate companies and tried to steer the thinking of these senior managers around to actively trying to influence the EVA for their companies since this was "the true measure of corporate success" (Stewart, 1991: 2). They argued that increasing earnings, earnings per share and return on equity is a myth when it comes to influencing analysts and investors. They argue that:

> Accounting measures of performance are only coincidentally related to stock prices and are not the primary movers and shakers. What truly determines stock price, the evidence proves, is the cash, adjusted for time and risk, that investors can expect to get back over the life of the business.
>
> (2)

The biggest impact that a company can have on EVA is to make managers in the business into owners. "To be sure, ownership must go beyond the merely monetary. It is first and foremost a question of attitude. Pride in one's work, sensible risk taking, and, above all, accepting responsibility for the success or failure of the enterprise are among the attitudes that separate owners from mere hired hands" (223).

Stewart developed the detail of the EVA approach and described different ways of analyzing company performance to show how the EVA approach might change perceptions. There was very little on the application of the approach other than advice on how to restructure calculations of performance. The principle way of adjusting management behavior according to Stewart was to make managers into owners.

The consultants, McKinsey, built on Stewart's approach, labeling it "Value Based Management" (VBM). They went further in describing the implementation approach and identified some key factors for successful implementation (Copeland *et al.*, 1995):

- Establish explicit, visible top-management support.
- Focus on better decision making for operating (not just financial personnel).
- Achieve critical mass by building skills in a wide cross section of the company.
- Tightly integrate the VBM approach with all elements of planning.
- Under-emphasize methodological issues and focus on practical applications.
- Use strategic issue analyses that are tailored to each business unit rather than a canned or generic approach.
- Ensure the availability of crucial data.
- Provide common, easy to use valuation templates and management report formats.
- Tie incentives to value creation.
- Require capital and human resource requests to be value based.

McKinsey said: "because true value-based management requires a change in mindset for decision makers at all levels, it is a long and complex process, usually taking around two years to achieve" (Copeland *et al.*, 1995: 116).

In each of the above approaches, implementation steps are prescribed in a detached, matter-of-fact, objectified fashion. In each case the steps to follow are set out in quite a clinical way with only Copeland *et al.* (1995) giving some hint as to the "complex nature" of introducing the value based management approach.

Evaluation of the measurement frameworks provided by consultants Coopers, Metapraxis and Nolan Norton, concludes that they were "strong on diagnosis and prescription, but somewhat vague about actual

implementation" (Geanuracos and Meiklejohn, 1994: 68). Implementation is portrayed as a "human relations challenge . . . which extends
from employee attitudes toward change to developing the right
organizational structure and providing the right compensation systems"
(Geanuracos and Meiklejohn, 1994: 68).

Less mechanistic views

Others take a much less mechanistic view of performance measurement
in suggesting that "any attempt to measure performance feeds back into
an organization and becomes a powerful influence on action itself"
(Eccles *et al.*, 1992: 145), and that "If managers fail to perceive a
coherent meaning behind a multivariable system [of measures] it may
lead only to confusion and a lack of focus" (148). This meaning is
created and shared through storytelling and rhetoric:

> in organizations there is a wide range of conversational practices that
> subtly inform the rhetoric of performance measurement. These
> practices usually include words such as authority, responsibility, and
> controllability. Through such rhetoric, managers propose theories
> about how performance measurement should be understood and then
> translate theories into practice.
>
> (Eccles *et al.*, 1992: 152)

The importance of the conversational perspective is also emphasized by
Quinn (1996) who argues that: "conversation is a basic characteristic of
the management task" (381) and has a fundamentally important place in
the implementation of strategy and its translation into performance and
its measurement. Bird (1990) introduced the concept of a "good
conversation" into the area of business ethics and the determination of
"the preferability of one course of action over another" (Quinn, 1996:
382). These "good conversations" are supposed to be reciprocating,
issue-oriented and rational in the sense that they are "intelligible,
reasonable and well-argued" (Bird, 1990: 39).

So, most of the performance measurement literature presents
prescriptions based on a linear view of causality of the "if-then" kind: if
you take the prescribed steps then you are likely to be successful. Others
point to the limitations of relying simply on systematic prescriptions and
emphasize the importance of storytelling and good conversations as
motivators. However, for them, good conversations are issue-oriented and

rational and implicitly, therefore, supportive of the drive to be "in control." Despite Kaplan's insistence that his approach to performance measurement is not about control, all of the approaches briefly reviewed above, including that of the balanced scorecard, use the language of being "in control" (Kaplan and Norton, 1996). The first step is always the formation, well in advance of action, of global intention as mission, vision, strategy or plan. There is an emphasis on prediction, clarity, sharing of values and perspectives, consensus and conformity. The whole approach assumes a world that is not paradoxical but in principle controllable, in which people can be relied upon to comply with the process if they are properly motivated. It is assumed that people will be motivated when they are involved in a democratic process of designing performance measures as rational, sequential systematic steps. However, evaluations of past experience of people in organizations trying to apply the prescriptions suggest that no one has been able to do it effectively or consistently for any length of time. I argue that this is because the kind of world being assumed is one sided. The approaches to performance management collapse the paradox of organizational life to the pole of "being in control" and so ignore the other pole of the paradox, that of "not being in control."

I now turn to my experience of Project Dashboard, comparing it to the prescriptions for implementing "balanced scorecard" and EVA measurements, thereby pointing to the paradoxical nature of organizational life characterized by aspects of being "in control" and "not in control" at the same time.

Project Dashboard

In January 1996, Geoff Ingles, head of the WSO at SB, announced the departure of two members of the leadership team: Roger Creighton, previous head of the WSO was to take a two-month break and join a Puerto Rican company; and Albert Peters, previous head of the technology group in WSO was to take a break and consider his next career move. Rumors abounded about things moving on, but no one knew to what. This was the background to the work of the Project Dashboard team. Part of my role in the team was to talk to site leaders about the proposed performance measures and report back to the leadership team, in accordance with the kinds of prescriptions set out in the previous section.

Conversations with site leaders

When I talked to site leaders about the proposed performance measures, they typically asked questions and made comments along the following lines:

> What do they want these for? Are they going to sit in the center of the organization and try to manage me? Of course we know that Geoff stands for control. He is trying to take away our freedom to act. Roger was good at giving us freedom to do things. He indicated what we needed to do and we got on with it. This new regime hasn't told us what it wants. If only it would tell us we'd get on and do it. Will these measures really tell us where we are going? What is it we are trying to achieve? How can these people micro-manage what we do in the plants from the center of the organization?

Such comments were then followed by speculation about what Geoff really wanted. The site leaders I spoke to seemed to be trying to work out what Geoff wanted so that they could start adjusting their positions and actions to fit in. When I asked them why they were doing this, they told me that the atmosphere in the organization had changed radically over the last year. "Whilst Geoff seems to want to encourage debate with himself over future strategy, he clearly doesn't want to listen to anything that doesn't fit with where he wants to go." "If I stand up and open my mouth on these things then I am going to be branded as somebody who doesn't support the new regime. If I keep my head down and just get on with things then I can survive. Later on we can adjust the operations to get back to where we were."

At the same time, however, there was a general acceptance that things must change so that SB would remain competitive. "We have achieved a lot under Roger and Geoff brings a fresh challenge. However, he seems to want to tell us what to do, rather than let us get involved in figuring it out." But, there was also fear of engaging in any challenge to the way things were at the time. Many of the site leaders were under intense pressure to deliver "stretch" performance goals. Most were trying to deliver two years' improvement in one year. They seemed to expect punishment to follow any failure to deliver. To deliver their targets, they sometimes cooperated with each other, but at other times they worked against each other. The very idea of reporting against even more measures was clearly experienced as threatening. "What will they do with this information?" "Surely the measures are supposed to show us whether we are achieving or not? But achieving what?"

After responses of this kind from site managers, I had a number of conversations with members of the WSO leadership team.

Conversations with leadership team members

In what follows, I give some indication of how some of these conversations went.

Person A

"Our Capital spends are out of control. We must get the capital in this business under control. People aren't managing their balance sheets properly. We don't know where our finances really are at the moment. The measures will get this thing under control. There has been too much focus on the customer service front in the organization. The inventory levels are too high and people can't tell me why. We are clearly paying too much for the service levels we are achieving.

"Sure the sites are trying to deliver from their perspective – but they are too focused on the local situation. We should manage the business by supply chains not by sites. It is key that we start to look at EVA returns on our assets and that we adjust our measures to do this.

"Geoff wants to pressure the business to deliver more. He doesn't know when he has squeezed too much though. We need the measures to tell us when we have pushed too hard.

"There is a team working on the strategic part of the plan. This would give us more of an idea of where we are going but we can't wait for them to deliver. Their timings have now slipped to October. We need to know where we are now. We can feed in the other stuff later on."

Person B

" I think I have some kind of rapport with Geoff. I helped him out once before when he was running animal health. Others let him down over that but I rescued him so I hope he will value me as a result. I also worked on a project that he sponsored and got on with him OK, so I hope that will help.

"This is not the time to directly challenge, though. We have to try to educate him so that he understands more about this business. He is under intense pressure from JP (Garnier) and Jan, though, to secure some significant performance improvements.

"We shouldn't forget what it was like when WSO first came into existence. We had to work hard to establish the organization. Geoff has got a hard time getting the commercial managers to support him. In fact they are challenging him. Although he is putting a lot of pressure on us, this, in a way, is not surprising because of the pressure he is under.

"There is not a consistent view of where we are going at the leadership team table at the moment. We don't have the strategic plan worked out yet. To a certain extent that is because SB hasn't got its overall position really well set. The CEO wants us to be a single enterprise but we really don't know what that means for us at the moment.

"As long as we continue to deliver then we will have some chance to influence things. On the influencing front it is important not to push too hard. Geoff is conscious that he has been relying on his old animal health team and is beginning to open up to others in the team, so doing anything that pushes them together again will not be helpful. We know, though, at present, that they are possibly the only routes to really get things through."

Person C

C. "Phil. I am very frustrated. I can't find the right questions to ask to unlock this thing at the moment. Maybe if we spent some time going through what we see at the moment it might help me to formulate something. I'm seeing Geoff on Monday and I want something to put in front of him to keep my conversation going with him."

PS. "OK" I jumped up and stood at the dry marker board. "Where do you want to start? What about where we think things are going at the moment?"

C. "OK. We are currently organized as factories reporting by area through to Geoff and we are engaged in the FIP project [factory rationalization]. I believe that we should be looking at the chains of supply as an opportunity for the future."

PS. "What about organization by product supply chain?"

C. "This may be something we get to. It could be constrained by overlap in the use of different pieces of capacity. At this point in time, though, I think that the chains are the transition piece. We might look at specific products later on. There is the strategic plan team looking at the future. This is a bit like deep thought, though. They are currently trying to analyze future demands and scenarios in order to come up with the approach we should take. This will be delivered as the answer 42, I expect, and then we will be left asking what the question was . . ."

PS. "How about Geoff then?"

C. "I met somebody the other day who had been at the Chemco managers meeting. Geoff had been speaking at the meeting and apparently had come over very well. People felt motivated by his comments. To me this suggests that he is beginning to connect with people and to get things moving."

PS. "This is interesting. I met someone else who had been at the same meeting. They said that Geoff had been complementary about some aspects of their business but then laid into them saying that they should be doing much better. He said that they should be focusing on some other things than they were. He took the view that they had not been contributing as much to the business as they might, and that they all had to try harder. This person reported that it was like they weren't being recognized for all their good efforts. This individual also reported that they were demotivated and threatened by the whole experience. He indicated that the group had not received the messages well."

C paused, "Maybe one way of making sense of this is that the person I spoke to could see a future for himself in the organization that Geoff would like to have. The person you heard from, Phil, maybe cannot see a future in the organization for himself."

PS. "Interesting way of looking at it. To me it tells us that the message reaching these people is mixed. Equally, people are reinforcing their perceptions of Geoff. One framework we have used in the past to look at this type of thing is the situational leadership model. In this case the organization could be considered as task immature in operating differently. It might be appropriate for there to be some form of centralization in the short term to direct things in terms of moving forward. In which case any shift back from delegation will be exaggerated, especially in this environment where many people seem to be feeling threatened. It also indicates there is no selling of a potential future going on in the organization or of any coaching of what people need to do or be in order to contribute. This is making for a very uncomfortable situation."

C. "What about Geoff himself? What sort of a person is he? Some time on this might help me with my approach?"

PS. "OK. For me I haven't seen him in action to form a firm opinion. The times I have seen him, he has been very challenging in his questioning of what has been presented to him. There is a picture of him in the organization as somebody who doesn't let people get close to him, who doesn't trust people, who doesn't provide much space for others to put their piece before he disagrees."

C. "Yes. It is almost as if he is hiding behind a mask. I believe he is somewhat insecure in the sense that he wants to win and doesn't know how to. He is under pressure at the top table. He is seen as coming to this role from what was seen as a second-class business and is now trying to establish a position of strength. He needs to do something radical to have an impact, though. It's much more difficult when you are in supply chain leadership. You are generally playing with small numbers with less impact on the business. So, big ego to satisfy, yet little to really shout about. He is a person who does not easily trust others. He also likes to play with models as long as you can show him their practical application."

"I think his bark is worse that his bite. The other day he told me that people think that he holds grudges. He doesn't. Once the fight has gone he forgets about it. So it is the perception that is left which is working against him. He also has a similar Myers Briggs to me – INTP – so I have a similar approach to things which is helping."

We ran out of time at this point. The board was covered with many drawings and representations used during the conversation, which went on for about two hours.

Person A (again)
Another meeting on another day:

I started by saying: "I believe we could do more with this measurement set. We seem to be designing it for short-term control. We need to bring it alive in terms of the organization seen as product chains too, so we can play with the outcomes and see what this information tells us. We can then start looking at how we want to use it. This will get us thinking about where we go with this concept."

A. "Phil, I like the sound of going ahead with this approach. Where would we get the information, though, on the chains? Won't it take us some time to do this?"

PS. "Two years ago there was a project started to create a manufacturing supply database. The owner of it lives three offices down from you in this building!"

A. "Wow! I never knew that. Give me their name. I'd like to have a look at this stuff."

PS. "One thing you will find is that the sites have progressed over time. They are beginning to organize in cells for production. One way of looking at our chains is to consider them as linked cells, rather than linked sites. I also believe we should look at specific products and play with those to see what we can get, rather than major chains."

A. "I am interested in doing this too. I feel that the major chains may still be too big."

PS. "I sense from your comments you want to get on with this. I had arranged to see PW (a consultant) to get this moving in March. I guess we could start earlier."

We also discussed the activities of others working in this area and the views that seem to be being developed. We touched on the future of WSO as being linked back into the total organization with no organizational boundary between supply, development and marketing/selling the products.

Was performance measurement really the task?

Somewhat to my surprise, during the meetings described above, I was drawn into conversation, time and time again, about the motives and behavior of the new leader of the organization. More and more people wanted to spend time on this, rather than the performance measures themselves. It seemed that I was engaged in a rolling conversation with people who were trying to make sense of their world in the context of this new man taking up the position at the head of the table. The task of developing and implementing the performance measures became almost incidental. The real project seemed to be a group of people trying to make sense of what was happening.

Clearly, the people I spoke to had become accustomed to the regime under Roger Creighton. Rumor had it that he was being removed for being too soft and undemanding on the cost front and letting too much go to the site leaders who, according to Roger's detractors, were being encouraged to run their sites as if they were their own businesses. Anxieties were running high, but what was driving the anxiety? People seemed to be trying to adjust their behavior in order to survive a perceived threat. The change of leader had generated a huge sense of the unknown, into which people seemed to be projecting some sense of impending doom, gloom and disaster. The new leader was being constructed, in the conversations in which I found myself, as some kind of fantasy figure. With virtually no first hand information, people were forming judgments and coming to conclusions, which in turn seemed to be affecting their behavior quite considerably. Furthermore, things seemed to be shifting, without any kind of plan at all, in the conversational exploration and sense making of the new situation. The fearful fantasy seemed to be one of a man sitting in an office, somewhere in the world, knowing all and dictating the next actions of everyone in the organization. This was thought to be the motive for the new performance measures. The very act of raising the topic of measurement in any conversation immediately triggered themes of "how can I stop this man taking control of me?" The fear seemed to be that new performance measures would expose activities that people wished to keep concealed, or at least wished to exercise their own discretion about. Themes to do with performance measurement triggered themes to do with control, which triggered themes to do with resistance, which in turn were subverting the approach to control through performance measures.

Running through the conversations I took part in, was the attempt to understand the intent of another so that there could be a matching of agendas without compromising basic beliefs and values. Suspicion seemed to surround Geoff. People feared he would use his hierarchical power negatively. Where intent was not stated then one was formulated and used to make sense of what was happening. One person made sense of Geoff's behavior in terms of the pressure being put on him by others, leading him to do the same. "Geoff has got a hard time getting the commercial managers to support him. In fact they are challenging him."

What struck me in this experience around performance measurement was the importance of activities to which we normally pay little attention, and upon which we usually do not reflect much, namely, the constructive role of ordinary, everyday conversation. Reflecting on the themes in those conversations, I can see how much they were expressing the sense of not knowing. People did not know what the new leader's motives were, for example. They did not know what the purpose of the new performance measurements was, or what the consequences of developing and using them might be. They kept referring, sometimes mysteriously and sometimes cynically, to the strategy team. All were waiting for it to pronounce on the future but those pronouncements never seemed to come, and in the meantime they had to carry on while not knowing what the future was or what the strategy for dealing with it would be. This experience of not knowing in relation to performance measures was part of a wider experience of not knowing more generally how the business was changing.

In this context of "not knowing," the purpose of the many ordinary conversations I took part in becomes clearer to me. It was in this communicative interaction that we were constructing meaning. What the change of leader and the proposal to employ new performance measures meant for people in the conduct of their roles was emerging in our talking together. Managers talk as much as they do because this is essentially the means they have at their disposal to construct new meaning in the midst of disrupted old meanings. Our ability to carry on doing our work in the midst of not knowing and so not being in control depends crucially on the conversations we have with each other.

In the last chapter I described a number of different conversational patterns. Sometimes conversation life takes on highly repetitive, stuck patterns in which new meaning cannot emerge. However, at other times conversation flows more fluidly, as we explore together the nature of the constraints on our actions and the potential for transforming them in creative ways. The conversations I have described in this chapter sometimes displayed the dynamics of "stuckness" as when people repetitively expressed their fantasies about the new leader. However, at other times conversations displayed a far more fluid dynamic, for example, as in those conversations in which themes of performance measurement were triggering themes to do with reorganization along supply chain lines. It was in these more fluid conversations that novel themes were emerging and taking the form of emergent intentions about changing the way we did business. Similar conversations, I know, were taking place in other parts of the organization. Intentions to do with moving towards a supply chain organization were being triggered and explored in many different kinds of conversation in many different places across the organization.

For me, then, it is in countless ordinary conversations in the living present, taking place in many local situations, that managers display the courage to cope with not knowing. It is in these conversations, as new meaning is constructed in the not knowing, that novel intentions emerge. Although we are not aware of it and take it completely for granted, as managers we live every day with the paradox of "not being in control" and of "being in control" at the same time and we find a way to do this in our ordinary, daily conversations with each other. It is there that we reconnect with disconnected meaning and it is in doing this that new intentions emerge. In our conversations, in many small ways we usually do not notice, the identities of our organizations and of ourselves are subtly transformed.

In the last few paragraphs I have been suggesting that the perspective of organizations as complex responsive processes provides a useful way of making sense of my experience of the events triggered by the suggestions of new performance measures. These complex responsive processes are conscious and unconscious communicative interaction and power relations in which people, in their relating to each other, construct meaning in their ongoing acting. A key aspect of the complex responsive process perspective is the centrality it accords to power relations and the way in which it understands power relations to be sustained and potentially shifted by underlying ideology. Another closely interlinked aspect of complex responsive processes of relating is the matter of anxiety. Disruptions to meaning opening up the threat of meaninglessness, the prospect of the unknown and the disturbance generated by shifts in power relations all provoke anxiety and this in turn triggers ways of dealing with it. I want to explore these aspects of ideology, power, the unknown and anxiety in relation to the intense concern people expressed about the nature and motives of the new leader.

Why the intense concern with the new leader?

One might look for reasons for all this concern with the new leader in the way he took up his role, especially in comparison to his predecessor. When the previous leader, Roger Creighton, first took up his position, he held focus group meetings and also many one-to-one discussion sessions, in which he talked and listened to those who wanted to offer him views on where the organization should go. Geoff, on the other hand, studiously maintained a distance between himself and others in the organization. So much so that he instituted confidentiality agreements with those working with him on significant projects. Put in place for legitimate reasons the very introduction of these agreements immediately suggested less trust than previously. On top of this, Geoff's natural tendency to avoid visits to production sites, and to work only with a small clique of people, seemed to feed the image of someone who was controlling from a distant center.

In the new regime people were reduced to studying the man from a distance, unable to really make sense of his intentions or needs through much direct contact. Feeling excluded they were then spending time and energy handling the implications of the negative images they had developed. A year into Geoff's tenure in his role much energy was still being expended on coping with him. The "reality" gap was filled with fantasy. Some people felt distant and disconnected. Those who had tried to connect and exchange their views with Geoff felt bruised and ignored in many cases. Some were hanging on to threads of a relationship: "I helped him out once so hopefully he'll remember this." Others felt more powerful because they really were close to Geoff and others knew this. They felt that they had some insight into what Geoff was really looking for and that they had some influence over what was happening.

However, it would be a mistake to ascribe the intense interest in Geoff simply to his personal style. What was being expressed in the conversations reported on above was a general phenomenon around leaders, probably exacerbated by Geoff's personal style and comparisons made between him and his predecessor. The general phenomenon I am referring to is that of power relations and the dynamics of inclusion and exclusion they generate. When a new leader takes up his or her role there is an inevitable shift in the pattern of power relations. Those who were close to the old leader, and so belonged to the "in group," experience some disorientation and may soon find themselves in the "out group." The new leader brings his or her own webs of previous relationships, many of which form a new "in group." This jostling for position, or at least the attempt to discover the new pattern of inclusion and exclusion, was evident in many of the conversations I have reported. The introduction into this context of a proposal to measure performance in a different way could only exacerbate the concern with shifting power relations and the impact of the dynamics of inclusion and exclusion. The performance measures came to represent, I suggest, a clash of ideologies.

Ideology and power

Project Dashboard with its emphasis on performance measurement clearly reflected the official ideology of hierarchical control through monitoring of facts and figures. The metaphor of a "dashboard" expressed a particular figuration of power relations in which the Leader of the WSO and his team were to be "in control" of the future direction of the organization through the action of selecting particular performance indicators and holding others responsible for achieving the targets set for those indicators. The unconscious purpose of ideology is to make the sustaining of a particular figuration of power relations feel natural, that is, to put current power relations beyond question. The implicit official ideology is one in which it is taken for granted that management is the activity of carrying out pre-given intentions, of controlling the activities of others, of removing uncertainty, of knowing. It is then perfectly natural for those higher up in the hierarchy to form intentions for the activities of those lower down and design procedures for ensuring compliance. In this way, power relations are patterned in hierarchical ways and communicative interaction is expressed in propositional themes to do with measurement of, and reporting on performance.

However, the conversations generated by the proposal to develop new performance measures were also clearly patterned by many other themes, often reflecting unofficial ideologies. Many site leaders were expressing largely unofficial ideologies in which it was taken for granted that site leaders should have the freedom to respond to unexpected local occurrences. These unofficial ideologies made it feel natural to oppose the imposition of what they saw as centralized controls. In other words, the unofficial ideologies render alternative figurations of power relations natural, and these are figurations in which there is a shift of power away from those higher in the hierarchy to those lower down. The advent of a new leader and the proposal to impose new performance measures threatened a shift in power relations from the periphery to the center, easily justifiable within the official ideology but justifiably to be resisted within the unofficial ideologies. These unofficial ideologies and their implied figurations of power relations tended to be expressed in narrative themes patterning the informal conversations I took part in.

From the perspective of complex responsive processes, communicative interaction between people in an organization is seen to have multiple aspects. These aspects are evident in the conversations about performance measures that I have reported earlier in this chapter. One aspect of the themes patterning our conversations can be described as formal, conscious and legitimate and this aspect is displayed in the propositional statements we made about the performance measures. For example, at some point in the conversation I would point to a definition of a particular measure and we would talk briefly about this in factual, analytical language. However, interspersed with propositional statements about the measure there would be questions about the reasons for the measure, which would soon trigger concerns about the new leader. It would, of course, have been quite unacceptable to talk in this way about the new leader in any formal setting. These aspects of our conversations were not legitimate in this sense and had, rather, the characteristics of shadow themes. It was legitimate to talk in ways that reflected the official ideology and the power relations it sustained but aspects of the conversation reflecting unofficial ideologies and thus tending to shift current power relations took the form of shadow themes. Some of these themes seemed to reflect fantasies about the new leader, expressing unconscious concerns. The ongoing conversations, with their multiple themes, simultaneously legitimate and shadow, formal and informal, conscious and unconscious, were themselves a process of making sense of what they were constructing.

In many cases the conversations I have reported constituted an activity in which people were trying to make sense of the consequences of their actions and decisions. They involved openly sharing thoughts and feelings in ways that rarely, if ever, occurred in the course of carrying out formal tasks. In these conversations, we were exploring each other's fantasies, off-the-wall ideas, and justifications for the things we were doing. We were accounting to each other. However, these conversations were not simply gossip, although that played a part. We were also, at the same time, carrying out tasks associated with the ultimate success of the business. And yet we were also exploring the motives, intents and actions of others. The tasks of the business cannot be separated off from personal matters or from implications for power relations simply because cooperative joint activity can only take place through human communicative relating. There can be no separation of purely rational actions and feelings and emotions of the actors concerned (Damasio, 1995). Sometimes I was surprised at what ensued when I initiated a discussion about what we were trying to achieve and what people felt about what we were doing. The unconscious and the shadow themes patterning our private, informal conversations are, for me, essential to what we do as people working in an organization. It is the form of relating we turn to, either in our own private conversations with ourselves, or in informal conversational exploration with others, to deal with our anxiety, insecurity, frailty and doubt, as well as to explore outlandish "what ifs" that may contribute to eventual change in our organization.

These conversations are characterized, to a significant extent, by redundancy in the sense that they are not directly related to the formal task of "creating economic value added," for example. However, I suggest that these redundancies, and the feelings that go with them, are important in achieving the formal tasks. This suggests a rather different perspective to that found in the literature on management networking, which draws attention to informal networks (e.g. Ibara, 1992; Monge and Eisenberg, 1987; Tichy, 1981), distinguishing them from formal networks in terms of their structure, and suggests that emergent networks develop out of "the purposive action of social actors who seek to realize their self interests, and depending upon their abilities and interest, will negotiate routinized patterns of relationships that enhance these interests" (Galaskiewicz, 1979). These studies tend to miss the simultaneity of formal and informal relationships and the intensity and quality of the relationships involved, which significantly influence the quality of the exchanges that occur.

The conversations that took place and views that were shared with me occurred quietly in people's offices behind closed doors to avoid the risk of exposure. Such conversations require relationships which have the quality of trust, and the capacity to live with anxiety. Coercive power raises anxiety levels and calls for greater trust before any disagreement can be expressed. The willingness of people to open up depends upon the perceived risks involved. Geoff's approach raised anxiety levels and thereby reduced openness and connectedness, making sharing more risky. This did not stop the process, however, which suggests that it is fundamentally unmanageable in the formal sense and potentially a key source of novelty and emergence in the organization. Creative sense making depends on qualities of conversation that enable fluid exchange and the coercive use of power may stifle the process or drive it underground as shadow themes organizing the experience of being together. Shadow themes are driven deeper underground when formal power tries to control them by blocking the flow of information, or is perceived to be threatening in some way. Participative sense making processes still continue but people become more guarded, reflecting the perceived risks involved, and to some degree are choosier in who they talk to. This connectedness is a fragile thing. Delicate tentacles reaching out to build new relationships may be pulled back in times of perceived threat. This reduces the variety of information to which an individual would be exposed in their interactions. Well-worn paths of conversation do not contain the same potential as those developed with somebody new. Somehow they lose their freshness. The opportunity for novelty to emerge seems to be lessened.

Conclusion

I have described the rich and complex nature of the activity going on in an organization implementing a balanced scorecard type measurement system. What is immediately apparent is the contrast between the clinical nature of the description of how to go about the task of implementation and the messiness of experience. The conversations accompanying the implementation of Project Dashboard brought out the uncertainty running through what might appear on the surface to be a straightforward exercise. However, everywhere I went, the process of making sense of what was going on had to be repeated, sometimes several times. What also became apparent was that the motives of the leaders of the organization were brought into question. This was especially in relation to the area of the maintenance, or not, of local autonomy and ability to stay in control of one's own destiny. Equally, each of the executives involved had a slightly different spin on the reasons for implementing the measures and therefore expressed the organization's strategy in a different way. The apparent difference between people's views seems to leave sufficient space for different meanings to emerge during the cascade implementation to those intended. This makes it almost impossible to achieve a position where all have the same clearly understood picture.

The experience of Project Dashboard points to the central importance of the conversations and of trust and connectedness in the context of developing the meaning for each individual involved, a point not really addressed by any of those recommending how to implement their measurement systems. Those affected by Project Dashboard wanted to express their views about the implications of the measures to their leader but the fantasy figure he had become in their minds prevented this. Because the literature says little about the messiness of implementation, it does not prepare implementers for what it will really be like.

In the end, what came of all this activity? Did we find the "right" performance measures and construct the "Dashboard" with which the leadership team could steer the business? The answer has to be: "not really." Did the strategy team, so often referred to, ever come up with the view of the future that people were waiting for? Again the answer has to be: "not really." So was it all a waste of time? I think not. In the course of talking about performance measures we were addressing many issues that were constructive in the emerging business situation, and an important part of that situation was how power relations were shifting, what people were feeling about this and how they were responding to those shifts. The theme of performance measures immediately triggered many other themes to do with performance in its wider sense and was quickly linked to themes, also patterning many other conversations, to do with supply chains and logistics. These conversations were part of a process from which emerged initiatives to develop supply chains as the basis for a reorganization of the business. What I have been describing is an ongoing process in which it is not possible to identify the beginning or the end. Instead there was a process in which meaning was emerging in the known–unknown of our business context and it was emerging in spontaneously self-organizing conversations. These meaning making conversations were the basis upon which we were able to undertake collaborative joint action.

From a mainstream perspective, it would be easy to dismiss what I have described as poor, confused management. Attention might be focused on Geoff's management style, and conversational activity seen as politicking and personal ambition, mere distractions from business objectives. This might then lead to easy prescriptions about appropriate management style and avoidance of emotion and personal politicking. The problem with this perspective is that it is a naive idealization which assumes that human beings can simply put aside their emotional and personal concerns to make simple choices about their personal styles. The naive assumption is that human beings can change their personalities and thus their behavior as simple matters of choice, no matter what the particular context. From an alternative perspective, however, namely that of organizations as complex responsive processes of relating, one focuses attention on the conversations I have described in a different way. Those conversations represent the courageous activity of continuing to relate to each other in situations in which we know and we did not know at the same time. Mainstream thinking focuses attention on management as an activity of controlling events (certainty) and when they appear to be uncontrolled (uncertain) this represents management incompetence. A complex responsive process perspective focuses attention on management as courage rather than control and that is the courage to live in the paradox of inevitable certainty and uncertainty at the same time. It is not through the impossible staying "in control" at all times that managers get things done. Rather, it is through the ordinary human courage of continuing to participate meaningfully, despite not knowing and despite not being in control, that managers get things done.

7 Supply chain management is messier than one might expect

- **The budget review meeting**
- **Mess in tension with order: meaning emerges**

In the last chapter I pointed to how themes in conversations around performance measures triggered themes to do with reorganizing the business along the lines of supply chains. In this chapter I want to provide an illustration from work on supply chain management as it evolved further in my part of SB. The literature on supply chain management defines supply chains as organizational systems for delivering products and services to customers, starting with suppliers' suppliers and ending with customers' customers (e.g. Blackwell, 1997; Gattorna and Walters, 1996; Poirier and Reiter, 1996; Ross, 1998). The chain is, in effect, an interlinked set of organizations, or operations, each supplying the other with information and products or services in order eventually to make a sale to a consumer. This definition leads to a practical emphasis on an integrated approach to logistics management with purchasing and materials management combined to work with production and finance functions. Andersen Consulting (1998) identified sizeable potential gains from more effective supply chain management but reported that larger companies (sales over £1 billion) were struggling to realize these gains. They identified specific areas for improvement and made the following prescriptions:

- Regularly implement strategies faster and more effectively than competitors.
- Define and utilize critical capabilities to their fullest.
- Launch and manage experiments since pilot projects could identify additional sources of value and implementation challenges to be overcome.

- Learn, adapt, and build from repeated success by following a "do, learn, do" model for implementation ensuring that people, processes, and technology are aligned with strategy and market conditions.

Managers at SB took up this kind of thinking about supply chain management and a new initiative, called the Enterprise program, was launched in 1996 with a view to improving supply chain processes across Worldwide Supply Operations (WSO) and Commercial Operations by the end of 1998. The key objective was to integrate and standardize the supply chain processes and systems, while adapting all systems for millennium compliance. Other objectives were to: link financial and volume forecasting so as to improve the quality of operational and financial planning; improve operational efficiency with the introduction of formal trading relationships between commercial and supply businesses; create an infrastructure to optimize plant to market flows. I was given a role in the Enterprise initiative and in order to convey some idea of my experience of participating in it, I want to describe an October 1997 meeting to review the Enterprise budget. I describe this meeting because, as a microcosm of the whole initiative, it illustrates the interactive process at play. In doing this, I am suggesting that it is in ordinary, everyday encounters between managers of the kind I will be describing that the shape of the whole supply chain reorganization and capability development emerged.

The budget review meeting

In October 1997, ten people met to review the budget for the Enterprise program or, as some put it, to "make sense of this damn thing and put forward something sensible to the chief operating officer." Colin Masterson, chairman of the international business said, "How did I get into this damn thing in the first place. I've got to go to my boss with this. He isn't going to be happy. Last year I told him it would be £12 million. Now it's more like £50 million." Tension and energy levels were high. "I want to go through this line by line. We've got to get it down to something more sensible. Equally, though, you guys have got to be confident that we can deliver. So, let's not screw ourselves."

Other participants at this meeting displayed varying degrees of commitment to the project and had their own individual anxieties about their reputations, credibility and career prospects. The other participants were:

- The president of corporate information resources (IR), whose aim was to try to standardize global systems.
- The chairman of WSO who also wanted this done so he could implement his global supply strategy.
- The Enterprise program director who wanted everything tightly planned and managed according to his project methodology.
- The vice president of IR development, who was behind schedule in delivering his part of the project and had already spent £2.5 million more than budget. He wanted to get his numbers accepted at the highest possible levels to cope with climbing resource retention and turnover costs.
- The vice president of Enterprise solution delivery, who was ambiguous about his participation in the project and had done as much as possible to evade any responsibility for delivery. Two months later he would go back to his job in European IR.
- The corporate finance vice president, who was there to ensure that his functional boss got what he wanted before he retired and also to curb the IR team who were, in his view, out of control.
- The supply chain logistics director who hoped to get this project to come to life.
- Finally, a senior partner from a consulting company who had much to gain in fees and much to lose in reputation if the project did not work.

We started the meeting by reviewing the IR development costs, soon focusing on an item of £6 million for a new approach to communications software. The original software approach, brought in from a previous project, had failed in testing and was then shown to be non-millennium compliant, so it was a write-off anyway. Knowing glances were exchanged as the finance representative turned up the heat on the IR team. Old differences were being raked over! In the end, it seemed, there was no other way forward. If we were to carry out the project then the communications software had to be budgeted at the higher figure: sighs of relief in the IR corner and more ammunition for the finance team at some future time. Finance promised to look at any potential overspends!

The program manager reminded us all that the scope of the project had not changed and that the old budget of £12 million was seed corn money anyway. He pointed out that this meeting was the first time anybody had even tried to assess the true costs of the project, which had been underway for almost a year. These remarks seemed to help Colin who was still very agitated at being the bearer of bad news to his boss. Others volunteered to help defend the position should he need it. The big unknown was what the business should be spending on this project anyway. "Have you got any comparisons?" was the question put to the consultant. "Not on this scale," he replied. Not much solace there, then!

"OK. Let's try to get rid of the SUN systems. We've already spent £400,000 on this development and got nothing yet. Can we take them out of scope and make some savings?" The group discussed this question. "I suppose its only 5 percent of the sales not included in the demand pattern," contributed one. "Yes. But if you don't get their inputs it can disrupt supplies to other parts of the business." Another said, "This is bloody difficult to assess without having some input from them."

Then the finance team's agenda became apparent. "We believe the company should go for standardizing on JDE and get rid of SUN." This was quite a change because they had advocated SUN for small markets only months previously. "Not possible at this time," said the IR team almost as one. "It's too close to the millennium to take the client server version of JDE." There was a pause. "We could just leave them as they are. How much is the cost to support these small markets again?" asked Colin. "About £1.2 million," came the reply. "Look. Since this would be a good step forward for these markets, perhaps we should argue to leave them in." The WSO leader nodded, "Yes. Key from my viewpoint." He really needed this if he was to improve supplies to these markets. "OK. It's worth a fight to keep it." So the meeting progressed.

Alliances formed and broke apart around various topics, as participants glanced at each other, sighed, and raised their eyebrows. Emotions flared and subsided as old scores came to the surface and receded and as new opportunities appeared from the background. There were those "I never knew that" moments, leading rapidly to "I told you so," and then some agreement around an issue, or some failure to agree. Sometimes there was a logical argument and then raw emotion and frustration: "I'll never get that one past him." Various anecdotes were produced to support first this and then that argument. Sometimes everyone tried to talk at once. There was laughter at a sudden joke and at the absurdity of the whole situation. There was giving and taking, and then total intransigence on some issue. There was table thumping to make a point strongly and then the unknown of whether we could really afford some item. Sometimes, interruptions completely changed the flow of conversation but at others Colin said, "We've started so we'll finish that."

Interspersed with all this there were questions, such as: can we find a new project manager? In the midst of conflicting interests, participants clearly desired to maintain credibility and power, while also making a difference. The conversation was characterized by tension and fear, by the deep resentment of some at "being stitched up," by the weariness of taking in all the inputs and managing all the engagements, by smiles, by frustration at the lack of progress and annoyance at not being heard, by the fear of having to justify a number you didn't develop yourself, by the joy of getting your point over, by the connections between some and disconnections between others. Sometimes there was a feeling of some kind of movement in the conversation and then we were stuck again.

Eventually a conclusion was reached. Somehow we had arrived at a number, £42.8 million, which seemed acceptable. Anxiety abated as the satisfaction of knowing that we had got somewhere, almost in spite of ourselves, settled on the group. Everyone had managed to get something of what they wanted and yet nobody had got everything. The outcome represented the transient sense we had collectively made of this project at this point in time in the context of the business in which we were operating. The arguments rehearsed in the review were written up to support the proposal we had agreed to put forward.

Mess in tension with order: meaning emerges

The conclusion was a cold number, supposedly hard evidence that could be used to manage the project into the future. In fact, however, the number was a shorthand, dense condensation of the discomfort, emotions, anxieties, alliances, surprises, facts and data that emerged in the interaction in the room on that October day. The number represented the pattern of meaning emerging in the project at that time as those involved in the meeting interacted with each other. Each acting on the basis of their own associations with the word *Enterprise*. These actions combined together to create a pattern of meaning which was sufficiently persuasive for Colin Masterson to feel confident enough to take to the Chief Operating Officer. This is an example of the wider process in which the supply chain initiative was under perpetual construction.

Each of those present, in their formal capacities and roles, were effectively signing up to delivering their part of the project. Each left the room still carrying different perceptions of what Enterprise was, as I afterwards discovered from individual conversations with four of the participants. On that day there was sufficient overlap of the individual meanings for a pattern to form around a budget number of £42.8 million.

From a mainstream perspective, this lack of a really shared meaning is seen as a problem. However, some of those writing from a perspective in the complexity sciences argue that it is micro-diversity of this kind that is essential for the emergence of new meaning (e.g. Allen, 1998). For me, the budget meeting described above is an example of self-organizing social processes in management. It highlights the emergent and dynamic nature of the manner in which those involved make sense of and act in the world in which they are working, a world they are co-creating in their conversations. The budget meeting was a messy experience in which we had to work with ambiguity, with little information, with not really knowing totally what we were doing or what the impact of our decisions would be. This contrasts strongly with the analytical/prescriptive flavor presented in the literature.

The self-organizing nature of conversation

Where does the pattern of order come from in the kind of management experience I have just described? One source is the roles managers have in the formal hierarchy and its formal processes. The budget meeting was part of the formal 3–1 planning process for managing the finances of the company. This legitimate control process utilizes analytical, rational planning tools. However this is only part of the overall process. Each individual brings different purposeful agendas. For example, the finance group intended to control the IR group. Individuals intentionally put forward proposals serving their individual requirements for success. Everyone intended to be credible and heads of individual business units intended to achieve their own particular and specific business goals. However, all were also prepared to compromise and none could know in advance what compromises would be required. Compromises were unpredictable responses to gestures made by others.

However, participation was not based entirely on hierarchical position. Although not explicitly stated, all were aware of who was an expert in a particular area and who is not. This did not preclude non-experts from talking but the subtlety of interpretation of technical terms meant that well-intentioned statements could be misinterpreted. Using the words without the knowing that goes with them can cause misunderstandings both of intention and of technical content. Generally, people do not like to check on words they do not understand in case they look as if they do not know what they are talking about and risk losing credibility with the others. Anxiety associated with not knowing can preclude some people from conversing on some subjects. This produces a self-organizing influence on the inputs and interventions made in the conversation, an implicit patterning.

The degree to which each participant is prepared to share also patterns the conversation. By providing rigid definitions of terms and making closed statements, some may find it possible to limit the scope of conversations about a particular issue. By challenging with open-ended questions or by making loose comments some may invite others into conversation or keep them out. This limits to some degree the options and alternatives being looked at. Again these devices provide a self-organizing patterning of the conversation. Individual perceptions of how a contribution might impact on personal credibility also affect what people say and so affect the emerging themes in the conversation. At SB there are some suggested ground rules for meetings that were brought to people's attention during the implementation of "Simply Better Way" (a culture change program implemented during 1993 in SB). Things such as: only one person should talk at a time; there should be an agenda with time slots, tasks and assigned people on it; a chairman should be assigned; a minute or note taker should be assigned; actions should be recorded and assigned with expected delivery timeframes; and side conversations should be limited. This structure is accepted to some degree, but ignored when people get really stuck into a discussion – this is what happened in the Enterprise review.

Clearly there was much ebbing and flowing of ideas and views throughout the meeting experience. It seems clear to me that nobody was in control of the meeting direction and outcomes. Eventually, we arrived at a "picture" of the project in which each of us could see enough that we could individually accept in order to be able to agree some kind of action plan. The general mulling and interaction that was going on was a necessary part of the meaning making process that we had to go through. It seems to me that it would not have been possible to analyze the individual views and opinions of those going in to try to predict the outcome. Equally, it is not possible to look at the outcome and say that it was one particular factor that, if controlled in some way, would bring similar outcomes elsewhere. The aspects I have been highlighting all point to the self-organizing, emergent nature of the conversation around the Enterprise budget.

So, it is in the process of interaction itself that is the source of pattern and that pattern is paradoxically regular and irregular at the same time. The interaction between embodied persons patterns itself in the turn taking/turn making interaction of ordinary conversation. The pattern takes the shape of themes that form the interaction at the same time as they are formed by the interaction. What I have described is a normal, formal meeting to review a budget submission that is to be made to senior executives. One aspect of our conversations there took the form of conscious, legitimate, propositional themes. The problem was clear, namely, how to deal with a substantial budget overrun. However, it was striking how personal ambitions and interpersonal rivalries also formed aspects of the process at the same time. These were not openly expressed in our conversations. Indeed, it would not be legitimate to do so. It would have been against the official ideology of putting emotion and personal ambition to one side and taking a rational, fact-based view. But of course, this did not mean that they were absent. There were clearly unofficial ideologies, which made it feel natural to express them in other ways. They were expressed as informal, often shadow aspects of our interaction. We all knew about these matters, even though no one voiced them. However, my story indicates the emotional undercurrents and the anxieties we felt. These were to do with not knowing just how realistic the figures were and how senior management was going to receive them. I think we were not all that conscious at the time of the anxiety and the impact it was having on us. In other words, there seem to have been unconscious themes patterning our experience of being together as a response to anxiety. The story also points to the way in which interaction between various patterning themes support or threaten current power relations. Even routine, rational activities of reviewing a budget, therefore, are patterned not simply in terms of formal, conscious, legitimate themes but also those that are informal, unconscious and shadow.

As I reflect on my experience of the meeting, I am struck by how:

- The available information on which we were to base our decisions was partial and inconclusive.
- Nevertheless, we continued participating in the conversation, in spite of not knowing. In this way, we co-created a pattern of meaning, which in turn triggered later conversations and activities in which the meaning further evolved.
- The budget was evolving in our interactions as the supply chain project itself evolved.
- The pattern of power relations emerged in our turn taking/turn making interactions with each other. Our conversations were characterized by processes of negotiating and personal risk taking.

- The pattern of conversation and the meaning emerging from it was organizing itself in our communicative interactions.
- We were living with the anxiety around knowing and controlling, finding the courage to carry on participating creatively despite not knowing and not being "in control."

The story also points to the nature of intention. We all arrived at the meeting with an intention, namely, to reduce the budget estimate. This was our response to the gesture made by senior management. Each of us also arrived with an individual intention, namely, to reduce our part of the budget as little as possible and hopefully even increase it. Whether this intention was realized, or not, depended on the responses they evoked from the others. These intentions and the responses they evoked were all themes organizing our experience together. It was relatively predictable that we would reduce the budget estimate. However, what we were all well aware of is that we would probably find ourselves in a similar position in the following year. After all, when we prepared the original estimate some time ago, we did not intend it to quadruple. In a sense we knew that what would happen over the next year would emerge, just as it did over the past year. The self-organizing interaction of the themes organizing our experience and the emergent nature of the outcome does not in any way mean that we were interacting without intention.

Furthermore, the purpose of the meeting was to fulfill our role in controlling the expenditure of our organization. But we knew that we had not succeeded in controlling expenditure since the last estimate and we also knew that this would probably happen again. Nevertheless, we did not take this as a cause for despair, entitling us to abandon the whole attempt. So we carried on seeking to make meaning. It would be a misrepresentation, in my view, to describe us as being out of control. This is the paradox of control again: in situations of uncertainty managers are "in control" and "not in control" at the same time.

Conclusion

Being simultaneously "in control" and "not in control" is exemplified by the Enterprise budget meeting. Each person arriving at the meeting considers the others to be competent, to greater or lesser degrees, in their roles. They vest in each other the notion that each is "in control" of their part of the project. Each has an implicit expectation that when another promises to deliver, they will. Those higher up in the hierarchy also implicitly assume that this team is in a position to control the project and its outcomes. The expectation is that the project is tightly managed to deliver on time and to budget and so improve the business. In one sense, then, managers are proceeding as if there is nothing paradoxical about control.

However, the paradox of control is revealed by the pattern of conversation at the meeting. Instead of being a clearly logical, crystal clear, straightforward management exercise, the meeting displayed all of these characteristics and their opposites at the same time. The supply chain may be neatly mapped out in boxes and defined so precisely that computers can be programmed to handle the information transfers required to make the processes work. However, the supply chain reality hits the same paradox as that reflected in the budget meeting. When a supply chain project is initiated it is discovered that every part of the chain has different systems and procedures. It turns out to be impossible to change each link in the chain at the same time to conform to newly designed standards.

The budget meeting reflected these problems. The paradox was highlighted by the underlying tensions, as people vied with each other to influence the pattern of conversation in the meeting. Each person taking part was in control of themselves, and they were playing the role of managers "in control" of the situation and yet they constantly questioned each other's motives, the information they possessed and whether there was time to get more. They made a "contract" to deliver and yet did not know if delivery was possible. The anxiety felt by the project leader, in having to find a way of maintaining his credibility with his boss in the context of being "in control" of this project, was clear from his comments. Eventually, the meeting ended with each having made their own personal meaning of events and with each going away to act on that meaning. What seemed like broad agreement and a joint contract was fragile, in the sense that none of those involved had made the same meaning and could act in ways to undermine the supposed agreement without even realizing it. It was as if the common view, so often sought by people to encourage aligned action, could, in fact, never be achieved. Since control of the project required common agreement, it follows that "control" in any simple sense was not possible. Paradoxically, then, the very process designed to bring about the control had within it the seeds of misunderstanding, which undermined the tightness of the control being sought. Effective managers, however, display the courage to continue living in the paradox.

8 Are managers "in control"?

- Mainstream understanding of control
- A complex responsive process understanding of the paradox of control
- Management as participating in the construction of meaning in the living present

If there is one consistent theme running through formal explanations of human organizations and prescriptions for their management developed over the past century, it seems to be this: organizations are the means that humans design in order to undertake the joint action required to achieve a given purpose. The formulations of scientific management in the early years of the twentieth century defined management as the tasks of organizing, planning and controlling. Prescriptions for the competent accomplishment of those tasks were given in terms of rational analysis of task requirements and human motivations to perform them. Success was equated with accurate prediction and the removal of uncertainty and conflict, so sustaining states of equilibrium. The development of systems theories applied to organizations over the second half of the twentieth century led to an enormous increase in the sophistication of thinking about management. However, the consistent theme continued. Organizations were thought to consist of interrelated subsystems, forming a system that interacted with its environment. The functions of management were understood to be:

- Designing subsystems and systems of joint activity having the capacity to adapt to the environment in a self-regulating manner.
- Setting the purpose of the systems in terms of goals, aims, objectives and performance targets and controlling the movement into the future of the organization as a system so that it achieved its purpose more effectively than others did.

The prescriptions for effective design, purpose setting and action control continued to rely on rational analysis, forecasting and the installation of negative feedback processes aimed at the removal of uncertainty and conflict to sustain equilibrium adaptation. Towards the end of the twentieth century, the systems dynamics strand of systems thinking was taken up and it pointed to the non-linear internal dynamic of human systems, with its consequent unexpected outcomes. However, the consistent theme continued. Organizations were thought of as complex non-linear systems of positive and negative feedback loops. The functions of management were now reformulated as:

- Identifying the positive/negative feedback structure of organizational systems, understanding the archetypal patterns generated by that structure, and then locating the leverage points where small managerial actions could have substantial effects on those archetypal patterns.
- Formulating visions for the future of an organizational system, a desired archetypal pattern, and operating at the identified leverage points in order to bring that future about. A measure of control over the movement of the system into the future is to be secured by controlling its dynamics.

Mainstream understanding of control

In what has come to be mainstream thinking, then, the movement of an organization into the future is the movement of a whole system from the present to the future. The essential function of management is to control that movement. To be "in control," managers objectively observe the system. They analyze it rationally in order to design it and/or identify and act upon leverage points in such a way that movement into the future realizes or unfolds a future state already enfolded in the present/past. The future state is enfolded in the system in the form of its design and the implied archetypal patterns of that design, in the form of the potential action at leverage points, and in the form of vision formulated for it. This is a linear temporal movement of the whole system from its past through the present into the future so realizing the chosen goals, or visions, and the paths to them intended/selected/planned by the hierarchically most powerful. As movement proceeds, variations from the path (gaps/errors) are detected and intentionally corrected, so sustaining movement approximately on the path. In short, managerial action forms the organization and its movement. This movement requires the human agents of the system to act in conformity and sustain consensus. The goal and the path are largely known and they are formed by management intention so that the movement of the organization is stable, regular, predictable and in principle certain. The movement expresses the identity of the organization as continuity, which implies the habitual movement of culturally determined behavior in which people share the same values. The resulting clarity is secured by conscious managerial decisions having the characteristics of formality and legitimacy.

In temporal terms, this whole way of thinking accords very little attention to the present. It relies on prediction, that is, the rational analysis of patterns experienced in the past and their projection into the future. In this sense the meaning of what people do is located in the past, formulated in the analysis of the past, or it relies on "visioning." This is an activity of an extraordinary, charismatic individual, in which case the meaning of what people do is located in the future as identified by the charismatic individual. The organization simply moves through the present but meaning is constructed in relation to the past and the future.

The opposites of all aspects of "being in control," such as reacting or responding as opposed to intending and planning, managerial action being formed by as opposed to forming the movement of the organization, uncertainty as opposed to certainty, not knowing as opposed to knowing, lack of consensus and conflict as opposed to consensus and conformity, are all to be removed by effective managers because they denote "not being in control." In mainstream thinking about effective management, there is no room for paradox. (The points made in the previous paragraphs are summarized in Figure 8.1.)

There are many examples of management research that have taken a descriptive rather than a prescriptive approach and in doing so, they point to a reality different from that assumed in mainstream theories and the prescriptions they lead to. There are descriptive studies drawing attention to the messiness of actual decision-making processes in organizations (e.g. Mintzberg and Waters, 1985; Lindblom, 1959; March and Olsen, 1976). However, the tendency is either to describe these processes in somewhat pejorative terms such as "muddling through" (Lindblom, 1959) or "garbage can" decision making (March and Olsen, 1976); or to present them as alternatives, such as *both* deliberate *and* emergent strategies in the sense that strategy is sometimes the former and sometimes the latter (Mintzberg and Waters, 1985).

Throughout this book I have been recounting my own experience as a manager at various hierarchical levels in organizations in contrast to the descriptive literature written by researchers who temporarily join an organization to describe it. This has been the experience of always participating with others in the paradox of intention and evoked responses at the same time. My experience is that of one communicatively interacting with others at all times in the known and the unknown at the same time. I would certainly not label what my colleagues and I were doing as "muddling" or as an inferior kind of "garbage can" decision making. I have been arguing for a way of thinking about the dynamics of human relating and joint action, that is, the dynamics of organizations, which is essentially paradoxical. This is the paradoxical dynamic of being "in control" and "not in control" at the same time. The apparently messy processes of communicative interaction I have been describing are not some second best but, rather, the only way we know of living with paradox. The very dynamics of organizational life call for the kind of complex responsive processes of relating that I have been describing. It is in these processes that the dynamic is created. The processes only appear to be messy and less than competent from the perspective of mainstream thinking about management. From the complex responsive process way of thinking, management skills and competencies lie in how effectively managers participate in those processes. They provide a way of thinking about what competent managers actually do to live effectively in the paradox of organizing, and what they actually do is continue to interact communicatively, especially in the medium of conversation, in spite of not knowing and not being simply "in control."

I want to distinguish the perspective for which I am arguing from two alternative responses to the recognition of the inherent uncertainty of organizational life. The first alternative is one of acceptance. This amounts to the call to embrace uncertainty, allow emergence to happen and accept that as a manager one does not know and one is "not in control." For me, this is the passive defense against living with paradox. It collapses thinking to one pole of the paradox. Such a response does not assist me in any way to make sense of my experience or to carry on working effectively in an organization. A manager who took this attitude would not last long in any organization I know of. In the accounts of my experience given in previous chapters there are a few examples of temporary resignation and even despair. But the next morning we were always back to work, actively trying to make sense of our situations and form intentions about what to do next. In all cases there were aspects of what we were doing that could be well described by all the words listed in

Figure 8.1 under the heading of "in control," and at the same time there were aspects that could be described by the words under the heading of "not in control." At no time did we simply accept the latter without simultaneously struggling to achieve the former.

The second alternative response to the recognition of uncertainty in organizational life is what I call the active defense against living with the paradox. This amounts to a call to "do it better" and "get it right." On recognizing that conversation is the primary medium of communicative interaction in which managers operate, some immediately turn to prescriptions for "good conversations," for "authentic conversations" and for special forms of conversation they call "dialogue." Good, authentic dialogue is defined as collaborative communication in which people suspend their assumptions and consciously hold themselves open to change. It is distinguished from ordinary discussions, debates and arguments, which are said to be competitive forms of communication in which people conflict with each other and seek to win. There are others, who, on recognizing the primacy of relationships, present prescriptions for managers to consciously behave in better, more caring ways. For me, these are idealistic hopes and in their emphasis on conscious design they collapse thinking to the "in control" pole of the paradox of organizational life. In all of the experiences I have recounted in previous chapters, I can see relating in which we were both caring and not caring, and I can see conversations in which we were collaboratively suspending our assumptions and competitively clinging to them, all at the same time.

The complex responsive process perspective, which I find makes more sense of my experience, is one that avoids collapsing thought to either the "in control" or the "not in control" pole. It avoids both passive and active defenses and sees organizational life as an exciting and anxiety provoking process of living with paradox. Here, managers are "in control" and "not in control" at the same time and they display the courage to continue participating in the making of meaning in paradox.

A complex responsive process understanding of the paradox of control

From the perspective of complex responsive processes, an organization is not thought of as a system but, rather, as interconnected patterns of action in time and geographic space. The perspective immediately shifts from that of an objective observer of an organization as a whole system to that of a participant in the living present of a local situation. The participant may be a chief executive, a senior manager, a supervisor or any other member of an organization. The living present has the temporal structure of gesture and response. Participants interacting make gestures to others thereby calling forth responses from those others, to whom they in turn respond in a continuous circular process. A gesture is thus simultaneously an intention (for example, a goal or an action aimed at achieving it, made by the most or the least powerful) and a response evoked or provoked by the preceding gesture of another, which was also simultaneously an intention and an evoked response to an even earlier gesture. Gestures and responses are thus simultaneously intended and evoked. This is the structure of all communicative interaction, including that of conversation. Participants in this circular process of communicative interaction are constructing meaning, which arises in the social act of gesture–response. The present is not a point through which an organization passes on its way from the past to the future, but a living process of communication in which the meaning of the gesture past is changed in the future response.

It is in this process of communicative interaction in the living present of local situations that managers and other members of an organization are perpetually creating its future. They are creating the movement of an organization into the future, as patterns of interconnected actions characterized by continuity and transformation at the same time. In other words, in their interactions in the living present, perhaps spread across many local situations, people are perpetually reproducing the identity of their organization and transforming it, if only in small ways, as they interact. Organizational continuity and transformation, identity and difference, emerge in the self-organizing communicative interaction of gesture–response. Such self-organizing local interaction in the living present has the intrinsic capacity to form and transform pattern. It follows that such interactions are characterized by the known and the unknown simultaneously. Furthermore, it is not organizational identity alone that is being perpetually reproduced and transformed but also the very identities or selves of the participants in the processes. We change in very personal ways as the organization we participate in changes.

The essential function of managers cannot be simply to control the paradoxical movement of continuity and transformation, of the known–unknown, because it is impossible for any participant to be in control of it. But this does not simply mean that managers are not in

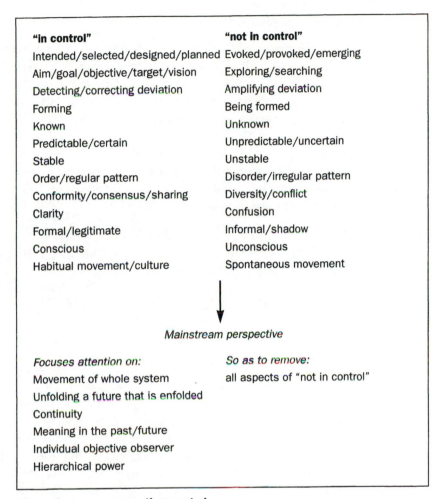

Figure 8.1 *The mainstream perspective: control*

control. Instead, managers are simultaneously "in control" and "not in control" in the sense that they intend their next gestures, which are simultaneously evoked by previous responses. There is coherence, which emerges as continuity and potential transformation of identity in the perpetual construction of the future. The movement of an organization is stable and unstable, regular and irregular, predictable and unpredictable at the same time. Managerial action forms the movement of organization while at the same time being formed by it. Potential transformative movement absolutely requires diversity of human participation as well as conformity, consensus as well as conflict, understanding as well as misunderstanding, all at the same time. All of this implies not only the habitual movement of culturally determined behavior in which people share the same values but also at the same time spontaneous interaction.

While mainstream perspectives focus attention on formal hierarchical power as the basis of conscious, legitimate decisions, the complex responsive process perspective understands power as simultaneously enabling and conflicting constraints that emerge in all human relating. Formal, legitimate hierarchical structures are simply one form of enabling constraint. Others emerge in informal communicative interaction, often patterned by unconscious and shadow themes, and together with constraints of hierarchical kinds, they form power figurations. Power figurations are sustained by official and unofficial ideologies and sometimes shifted by the latter.

Complex responsive processes of relating are processes of communicative interaction in local situations, with their gesture–response structure of the living present, in which meaning is reproduced and potentially transformed. The inevitable companions of these processes are the excitement of participating in the construction of meaning and the anxiety that the potential loss of meaning provokes. Together they constitute the feeling of being alive.

This perspective leads to a different understanding of the nature of management. It becomes misleading to equate management with being "in control" because this is simply one pole in the paradoxical experience of managing. Instead, the key to the nature of managing an organization lies in courage. By courage I do not mean the heroic version in which an individual confronts and overcomes something fearful. Rather, I mean the courage to carry on participating creatively with others in the construction of meaning, despite not being "in control." This amounts to the courage to live with paradox and the anxiety generated by the potential loss of meaning. Anxiety is to be distinguished from fear. The latter has a clear object. We know what we are afraid of and what we therefore need to confront and overcome. Anxiety, on the other hand, is a general state of unease for which no causal object can be identified. The anxiety relates to a general sense of something amiss, an unconscious sensing of the potential loss of meaning. The courage of management in the sense of finding the capacity to carry on participating is not simply an attribute of a lone individual but a quality of participation with others. The distinctive competence of the manager, therefore, becomes the skill of participating effectively with others in processes in which new meaning potentially emerges in the midst of the meaning destroying changes encountered. This participation is a process in which not only the identity and transformation of an organization emerges but one in which the identity of those participating also emerges as continuity and potential transformation. Such participation is therefore deeply personal and relationship dependent. It cannot be simply a rational procedure but must always involve emotion and will always have unconscious as well as conscious aspects.

The distinguishing feature of management is not control but courage. The points made in the previous paragraphs are summarized in Figure 8.2.

Management as participating in the construction of meaning in the living present

The central notion of mainstream thinking, that of the manager being "in control," is therefore much more problematic than is usually assumed because managers are both "in control" and "not in control" at the same time. The key question then becomes how organizations operate effectively and maintain reasonably orderly states of affairs if their managers are not simply "in control." From the perspective of complex responsive processes, it is transiently stable, self-organizing patterns of meaning that maintain a sense of order and therefore a sense of control as managers go about their daily activities. Intentional goal-oriented acts emerge in the conversations of managers at a local level and those conversations function as patterning, meaning making processes. These communicative interactions constitute the way in which managers, individually and collectively, maintain their sense of self and their defenses against anxiety. An organization is self-organizing processes in which intention and meaning emerge and anxiety is lived with. These interconnected processes across an organization generate collective emergent outcomes that cannot be traced back to specific actions. Processes of change and performance achievement emerge in the self-organizing patterns of meaning in which each individual struggles, in participation with others, to maintain a sense of self in an uncertain world. This is the process of an organization's evolution.

This emergent pattern of evolution arises in self-organizing interaction and creates a felt sense of meaning, order or control in the midst of uncertainty and anxious feelings of "not being in control." The paradox of being "in control" and "not in control" at the same time pervades all hierarchical levels in the organization: the individual; individuals in

"in control"	"not in control"
Intended/selected/designed/planned	Evoked/provoked/emerging
Aim/goal/objective/target/vision	Exploring/searching
Detecting/correcting deviation	Amplifying deviation
Forming	Being formed
Known	Unknown
Predictable/certain	Unpredictable/uncertain
Stable	Unstable
Order/regular pattern	Disorder/irregular pattern
Conformity/consensus/sharing	Diversity/conflict
Clarity	Confusion
Formal/legitimate	Informal/shadow
Conscious	Unconscious
Habitual movement/culture	Spontaneous movement

Complex responsive process perspective

Movement in local situation, self organization/emergence perpetually constructing the future. Movement of paradox as gesture–response

Simultaneous continuity and potential transformation. Identity and difference

Meaning in the living present

Participation in subjective interaction in groups

Power as emergence of enabling constraints, including hierarchical constraints, ideology and dynamics of inclusion/exclusion

Anxiety and courage

Figure 8.2 *The complex responsive process perspective: the paradox of control*

conversation; the department level; the business unit level; the corporate level; and the industry level.

From a mainstream perspective, what I have just described would be interpreted as management incompetence. Indeed, this is just how, at first, I thought about the merger described in chapter three. The question that nagged me was: how could the apparently competent top management team have got the business into such a mess that it had to merge to survive? The only answer, when I took the mainstream perspective, was that the top team was incompetent. They should have been able to ensure predictable outcomes and maintain a hold over the development of the organization. They should have been able to anticipate important potential changes and put in place controls to ensure that only the intended outcomes were realized. However, the more I got involved, the more I saw that managers are always working with only part of the picture. There is always information missing that somehow, afterwards, turns out to be of major importance.

But should we not have kept asking questions until we had a full grasp of events before we acted, thereby ensuring that outcomes were achieved in a less messy way? The accounts of my experiences in previous chapters suggest that this is a naive question. As a practicing manager, I was working with many colleagues in the experiences described. All of us were committed to further the interests of the organization in which we worked. Generally speaking our purpose was to move the company along a path chosen by the company's top executives in line with their assessments of the future needs of the business in order to bring about our collective success. All of us were constantly involved in making sense of what was happening in the corporation as a whole. We were constantly having to exercise judgments about what was the most appropriate action in the circumstances in which we found ourselves in order to further contribute to the achievement of the goals of the business as we understood them. We did what we could to the best of our abilities in a fast changing situation. To suggest that we could have taken more time, that we could have done more research and thinking, is to miss the dynamic nature of the practice of management.

Instead of thinking in terms of sequential thought before action, it now makes more sense to me to think of my experiences in terms of a fundamental dynamic manifesting itself in an organizational context. This dynamic is the self-organizing emergence of meaning that takes place constantly in social interactions and conversations. It is present in all circumstances in the social interactions in an organization. The stress and anxiety experienced in coping with this dynamic is borne by everyone in an organization, not just the managers, but by all members of an organizational community. I would argue that it takes a high degree of competence to make sense of the patterns emerging in this dynamic process of interaction and self organization. The ability to generate personal meaning from this dynamic underpins the ability to act effectively into the emerging pattern, thereby creating what happens next, but without knowing what will happen next.

This book began with the search for an answer to a simple, yet important question: are managers in control of organizations in which they work? My experience now suggests to me that this is the wrong question. The key management ability is not that of being "in control" but the ability to participate creatively in the formation of transient meaning, which enables all of an organization's members to continue living with the anxiety generated by change. It is this meaning that creates a felt sense of order, coherence, pattern or control. The ability to participate creatively in the construction of meaning develops as managers struggle to cope with the paradox of control, using legitimate control mechanisms as tools in a wider dynamic of self-organizing communicative interaction. I believe that management practitioners continually hone and develop the capacity to live with paradox as they go about their practice, even if they are not all that aware of doing it. It is, therefore, an ability that the practitioners come to know through the sense they make of their experiences and not something that can be distilled into propositional statements to be taken apart and analyzed to determine the best way to pursue it. I would suggest that as anxiety levels rise we sense a loss of control, the order that was helping us to feel safe begins to dissolve, and we begin to search for new senses or meanings in order to reassert self control. The search for new or different patterns that make more sense to us is, I believe, a largely unconscious process and it is self-organizing in nature. We feel rising anxiety levels in the form of discomfort, which may drive us into communicative acts as parts of the search. Or, too much anxiety can drive us to fall back into ourselves in an attempt to shut out the flow as we feel complete lack of any ability to reassert control over events. These are the dynamics of managing.

This leads to the crucial distinction between mainstream thinking and the perspective I am proposing. Mainstream thinking focuses attention on management intention, which it takes for granted, and on the systems required for staying in control. The perspective I am proposing focuses attention on the wider self-organizing dynamic in which managers participatively construct meaning and in which intention emerges. Some of the tools they use in this process are systems of control. However, the essential management capacity is the courage to participate in the construction of meaning in spite of not being "in control."

What is the advantage of taking this alternative perspective? When I try to make sense of what I do as a manager from the mainstream perspective, I continually experience the frustration of feeling that I am not good enough because the control I am supposed to exercise never seems to materialize as it should. This increases my anxiety and reduces my capacity to participate creatively. When I take the alternative perspective, I come to understand and value much more the confusing struggle I am engaged in with others to make sense of what is happening to us and what we are doing. I come to see that this is how we get things done and my feelings of frustration, disappointment and incompetence diminish. I come to enjoy the struggle to find meaning and this reduces anxiety levels, so enhancing my capacity to carry on participating creatively in spite of not being "in control." I come to pay more attention to important participative processes, which I hardly even noticed before and this, I believe, makes me a more effective manager, not one who is always "in control" but one who is "good enough."

The "good enough" manager

What are the attributes of "good enough" managers? Such people are able to accept their own frailty in the face of all the expectations and projections of others, which imply that they are uniquely "in control" of events and all knowing. Through their belief in themselves these people are able to participate actively in creating a context that enables much greater degrees of connectedness and trust between people. This is important for the expression of shadow themes organizing experience in organizations. The skill seems to be an ability to contribute to the reduction of anxiety, which enables more meaningful conversations. The motivating force for the search for new meaning in the social interactions in the organization seems to be the expression of identity and this is linked to control and anxiety. An increasing sense of loss of control increases anxiety levels and seems to drive up the search for new patterns of meaning. Too much anxiety can shut down the search as people reduce the level of interconnection as part of their own defense strategies. Similarly perceptions of an increasing sense of order, or control, seems to inhibit the search for new patterns by reducing the levels of anxiety to a point where there is insufficient energy to "move."

The continuous process of making and remaking patterns of meaning, which is the organization, takes place in the conversations of the participants and it has a life of its own. This is the emergent, self-organized sense of organization that people working within it carry with them through their working day. They co-evolve as they interact while going about their business. The patterns that emerge are stabilized in institutionalized ways of working and then become recorded in procedures and structures as a route to reducing the inherent uncertainty of carrying out the activity. These habitual patterns also emerge in conversation and behavior as "culture." Once a "culture" has emerged, mainstream thinking tends to objectify it and then advocates the intentional management of culture. However, if one understands culture as the habitualization of themes that emerge in conversation, then one has to conclude that it is impossible to manage culture.

Conversation, connectedness and information

The experiences recounted in previous chapters have highlighted the importance of conversation in sustaining the transient sense of organization and individual identity. The quality of conversation appears to be a key factor in the evolution of an organization. The "depth" or intensity of a relationship seems to be important in the level of connectedness reached in conversation, impacting the quality of what is constructed both in words and in feelings. Perceptions of the depth of relationships, usually built on trust, seem to be important in terms of the weight given to particular views and to the sense derived in particular encounters. A fundamental aspect of the most intimate exchanges in conversation is the perception of trust in relationship. For me, this is based on emotional "evaluations" made by those involved. These seem to be both at the conscious and unconscious level, as we adjust the extent to which we share with the other on the basis of evaluations of the threats or risks involved.

The patterns of conversation, and therefore meaning making, at SmithKline Beckman and SmithKline Beecham were not purely random in nature. Something was driving people to engage with each other and converse as they did. I am suggesting that the interactions were at least, in part, driven by a search for patterns of meaning to provide sufficient sense of situations thereby generating the basis for actions. I am carefully avoiding suggesting that some overarching, collective, explicitly agreed and understood mission, or higher ideal is driving people's behavior, since I do not believe that this was the case in any of the experiences I have described. I am also proposing, therefore, that the continual search for meaning through conversation is central to the dynamic processes that produce transiently stable patterns, which give rise to an emergent sense of order.

Anxiety

The view of managers encouraged by mainstream thinking is that they are rational planners and unemotional builders and maintainers of organizational systems. Rarely do the underlying feelings of people in management roles merit exploration or examination. The works of those associated with the human relations movement (e.g. Mayo, 1933; Roethlisberger and Dickson, 1939) explored the motivation of people at work, but still within a view of management that assumed an objective reality and was very much associated with being "in control" and providing leadership on this basis. This assumption pre-empts the examination of a prime driver of the continual struggle to make sense of the world in which we participate, namely, the anxiety arising in the uncertainty inherent to management.

In the individual, anxiety levels rise or fall depending upon the perceived level of control they have over themselves or their environments. I am suggesting that to make sense of the experiences I have related we need to consider the energy for searching for new meaning as arising from differing levels of anxiety felt both within and between individuals who are interacting at work. Anxiety is therefore ever present, reflecting the continual threat of collapsing into disorder and chaos. In tension with this is the search for stable patterns of meaning that comes from the recognition of order and the sense of control, which alleviates anxiety. The tension between the stable and the unstable, the ordered and the disordered, the self and other, and the meaningful and meaningless is experienced as anxiety. I am suggesting that this could be a source of the energy that drives those involved to search for a new and different meaning of the world and their place within it. The presence of anxiety is therefore normal, healthy and essential for the emergence of novelty and change in the work environment.

Conclusion

It seems to me that the notion of being "in control" must be distinguished from a sense of coherence in experience. There seems to be a tendency to mix these two separate notions up. Perhaps this happens because, as individuals, it is important to us to preserve a sense of self as being "in control," which we then project onto the world we live in. There seems to be a tendency in our culture to move too easily from the perception of order in the world to the assumption that one can control it. The struggle to retain a sense of self in relation to others, to hold on to a sense of order is linked to the need to keep at bay the anxieties associated with disorder and unpredictability. Perhaps this is a fundamental motivator in the search for meaning, one that drives our need for connection and conversation in the organizational context. In these conversations we create a sense of order but because of the way we think this seems insufficient. So, in our anxiety we are ready to believe that someone, somewhere, is "in control." However, the notion of the manager as one who is in control is not consistent with experience. Instead, managers find that they have to live with the paradox of being "in control" and "not in control" simultaneously. It is this capacity to live with paradox, the courage to continue to participate creatively in spite of "not being in control" that constitutes effective management.

Postscript

As if to reinforce all of my experiences over the years working in SmithKline Beecham a new conversation emerged during 1998 and continued throughout 1999 about the need to address the scale of the company in the context of a consolidating pharmaceutical industry. This led to the merger with Glaxo Wellcome announced in January 2000 and finally completed at the end of December 2000. During 2000 I was involved in merger related activity and engaged in new conversations and experiences with my new colleagues at Glaxo Wellcome, developing the thinking for the supply chain organization and logistics processes for GlaxoSmithKline. I also turned 40 years old and began to reflect even more about my experiences and the insights I have gained through doing this work. I began to talk with others about this both inside and outside the company. This eventually led me to several conversations with people from other companies about opportunities there and finally to a dilemma. Do I accept the offer of a new job within GlaxoSmithKline or do I join the board of a Kingfisher subsidiary company and leave SmithKline Beecham?

As I have come to understand more about what I have been engaged in as a manager and more about myself as a person, I have discovered a whole new paradoxical world to explore. This world values differences and interaction with new people. I have come to value the experience of working with many others in coping with paradox. It is an exciting and rewarding thing to do. I felt, therefore, that changing industries and companies would be a way to continue this exploration and so took the plunge to join Entertainment UK as Supply Chain Director. In doing so I wished all of my friends and colleagues at SmithKline Beecham good luck with all of the anxieties and uncertainties that a merger brings.

Ironically, six weeks after handing in my notice, and while still serving my notice period out at SmithKline Beecham, the Kingfisher Group announced that it was to demerge and create New Kingfisher and a General Merchandise company. By the time I started my new job I was entering into an organization trying to come to terms with this stated intention. It only goes to show that managing really is an endless task of engaging in new conversations and opportunities with all of the anxieties and uncertainties that they bring!

References

Ackoff, R. L. (1970) *A Concept Of Corporate Planning*, New York: Wiley.

Aguago, R. (1991) *Dr. Deming: The American Who Taught The Japanese About Quality*, New York: Simon & Schuster.

Allen, P. M. (1982) "Self-Organisation in the Urban System", in Schieve, W. C. and Allen, P. M. (eds) *Self-Organisation and Dissipative Structures. Applications in the Physical and Social Sciences*, Austin: University of Texas Press.

Allen, P. M. (1998) "Evolving Complexity in Social Science" , in Altman, G. A. and Koch, W. A. (eds) *Systems: New Paradigms for the Human Sciences*, Berlin: Walter de Gruyter.

Andersen Consulting (1998) *Integrated Supply Chain Management – Work in Progress*, London: Andersen Consulting.

Anderson, J. C., Rungtusanatham, M. and Schroeder, R. G. (1994) "A Theory of Quality Management Underlying the Deming Management Method," *Academy of Management Review* 19 (3): 472–509.

Arthur, W. B. (1988) "Self Reinforcing Mechanisms in Economics," in Anderson, P. W., Arrow, K. J. and Pines, D. (eds) *The Economy as an Evolving Complex System*, Reading, MA: Addison-Wesley.

Bakhtin, M. M. (1986) *Speech Genres and Other Late Essays*, Austin: University of Texas Press.

Balloun, J. and Gridley, R. (1990) "Post-merger Management: Understanding the Challenges," *The McKinsey Quarterly* 4: 90–102.

Barley, S. R., Meyer, G.W. and Gash, D. C. (1988) "Cultures of Culture: Academics, Practitioners, and the Pragmatics of Normative Control," *Administrative Science Quarterly* 33: 24–60.

Bastien, D. T. (1987) "Common Patterns of Behaviour and Communication in Corporate Mergers and Acquisitions," *Human Resource Management* 26 (1): 17–34.

Bauman, R., Jackson, P. and Lawrence, J. (1997) *From Promise to Performance*, Boston: Harvard Business School Press.

Becker, S. (1993) "TQM Does Work: Ten Reasons Why Misguided Efforts Fail," *Management Review* 82 (5): 30–34.

Bird, F. (1990) "The Role of 'Good Conversation' in Business Ethics," in

Proceedings of the First Annual James A. Waters Colloquium on Ethics in Practice, Chestnut Hill, MA: Boston College Management School.

Blackwell, R. (1997) *From Mind to Market*, London: Harper Business.

Boje, D. (1991) "The Storytelling Organisation: A Study of Story Performance in an Office-supply Firm," *Administrative Science Quarterly* 36: 106–126.

Boje, D. (1995) "Stories of the Storytelling Organisation: A Postmodern Analysis of Disney as 'Tamara-Land'," *Academy of Management Journal* 38 (4): 997–1035.

Bowen, D. E. and Lawler, E. E. (1992) "Total Quality-oriented Human Resources Management," *Organisational Dynamics*, (Spring): 29–41.

Box, E. P., Hunter, W. G. and Hunter, J. S. (1978) *Statistics for Experimenters: An Introduction to Design, Data Analysis, and Model Building*, New York: John Wiley.

Brocka, B. and Brocka, M. S. (1992) *Quality Management: Implementing the Best Ideas of the Masters*, Homewood, IL: Irwin.

Broedling, L. A. (1990) "Foreword" in Varian, T. (ed.) *Beyond the TQM Mystique: Real-World Perspectives on Total Quality Management*, Washington DC: American Defence Preparedness Association with Organisational Dynamics.

Brown, J. S. and Duguid, P. (1991) "Organizational Learning and Communities of Practice: Toward a Unified View of Working, Learning and Innovating," *Organizational Science* 2(1): 40–57.

Buono, A. F. and Bowditch, J. L. (1989) *The Human Side of Mergers and Acquisitions*, San Francisco: Jossey-Bass.

Burdett, J. O. (1991) "How to Build a Business Network," *Executive Development* 4 (4): 8–9.

Burt, R. S. (1982) *Toward a Structural Theory of Action*, New York: Academic Press.

Cabrera, J. C. (1985) "Take-overs . . . The Risks of the Game and How to Get Around Them," *Management Review* 71 (11): 17–21.

Carter, C. and Williams, B. (1957) *Industry and Technical Progress*, Oxford: Oxford University Press.

Choi, T. Y. and Behling, O. C. (1997) "Top Managers and TQM Success: One More Look after All these Years," *Academy of Management Executive* 11 (1): 37–47.

Chorn, N. H. (1991) "Total Quality Management: Panacea or Pitfall?," *International Journal of Physical Distribution and Logistics Management* 21 (8): 31–35.

Collins, B. and Huge, E. (1993) *Management by Policy: How Companies Focus their Total Quality Efforts to Achieve Competitive Advantage*, Milwaukee, WI: Quality Press.

Cook, K. S., Emerson, R., Gilmore, M. R. and Yamagashi, T. (1983) "The Distribution of Power in Exchange Networks: Theory and Experimental Results," *American Journal of Sociology* 89: 275–305.

Copeland, T., Koller, T. and Murrin, J. (1995) *Valuation: Measuring and Managing the Value of Companies*, New York: John Wiley & Sons, Inc.

Costello, T. W., Kubis, J. F. and Shaffer, C. L. (1963) "An Analysis toward a Planned Merger," *Administrative Science Quarterly* 8 (2): 235–249.

Crawford, C. M. (1991) *New Products Management*, Boston: Irwin.

Damasio, A. R. (1995) *Descartes' Error*, London: Picador.

Davis, B. L., Gebelein, S. H., Hellervik, L. W., Sheard, J. L. and Skube, C. J. (1992) *Successful Manager's Handbook*, Minneapolis, MN: Personnel Decisions Inc.

Deming, W. E. (1982) *Quality, Productivity and Competitive Position*, Cambridge, MA: MIT Press.

Deming, W. E. (1986) *Out of the Crisis*, Cambridge, MA: MIT Press.

Deming, W. E. (1993) *The New Economics for Industry, Government and Education*, Cambridge, MA: MIT Press.

DiMaggio, P. (1992) "Nadel's Paradox Revisited: Rational and Cultural Aspects of Organisational Structure," in Nohria, N. and Eccles, R. G. (eds) *Networks and Organisations: Structure, Form and Action*, Boston: Harvard Business School Press.

DiMasa, J. A., Hansen, R. W., Grabowski, H. G. and Lasagna, L. (1987) "Cost of Innovation in the Pharmaceutical Industry," *Journal of Health Economics* 10: 107.

Doyle, K. (1992) "Who is Killing Total Quality?," *Incentive* 16 (8): 12–19.

Drews, J. (1989) "Research in the Pharmaceutical Industry," *European Management Journal* 7 (1): 23–30.

Drucker, P. F. (1986) *Innovation and Entrepreneurship*, London: Pan Books.

Durman, P. (1998) "Drug Companies Warned to Hone R&D," *Times*, November 12, 1998: 35.

Eccles, R. G., Nohria, N. and Berkley, J. D. (1992) *Beyond the Hype: Rediscovering the Essence of Management*, Boston: Harvard Business School Press.

Economist (1992) "TQM Survey," *Economist*, April 18, 1992: 67.

Elias, N. and Scotson, J. (1994) *The Established and the Outsiders*, London: Sage.

Fombrun, C. J. (1982) "Strategies for Network Research in Organisations," *Academy of Management Review* 7: 280–291.

Fonseca, J. (forthcoming) *Complexity and Innovation in Organizations*, London: Routledge.

Fried, Y., Tiegs, R. B., Naughton, T. J. and Ashforth, B. E. (1996) "Managers' Reactions to a Corporate Acquisition: A Test of an Integrative Model," *Journal of Organisational Behaviour* 17: 401–427.

Frost, P. J. and Egri, C. P. (1991) "The Political Process of Innovation," *Research in Organisational Behaviour* 13: 229–295.

Galaskiewicz, J. (1979) *Exchange Networks and Community Politics*, Beverly Hills: Sage.

Gattorna, J. L. and Walters, D. W. (1996) *Managing the Supply Chain*, Basingstoke: Macmillan Press.

Geanuracos, J. and Meiklejohn, I. (1994) *Performance Measurement: The New Agenda – Using Non Financial Measures to Improve Profitability*, Wimbledon: Business Intelligence.

Gell-Mann, M. (1994) *The Quark and the Jaguar*, New York: W. H. Freeman & Company.

Grabowski, H. and Vernon, J. (1984) "A Computer Simulation Model of Pharmaceutical Innovation," in Lindgren, B. (ed.) *Pharmaceutical Economics*, Stockholm: Liber Forlag.

Grove, A. S. (1996) *Only the Paranoid Survive*, London: HarperCollins Business.

Gupta, A. and Wilemon, D. (1990) "Accelerating the Development of Technologically Based New Products," *California Management Review* 32 (Spring): 24–44.

Hall, N. (1997) "A Landmark in Drug Design," *Chemistry in Britain* 33 (December): 25–27.

Halpern, P. (1983) "Corporate Acquisitions: A Theory of Special Cases? A Review of Event Studies Applied to Acquisitions," *Journal of Finance* 38 (2): 297–317.

Hanks, W. F. (1994) Foreword to Lave, J. and Wenger, E., *Situated Learning: Legitimate Peripheral Participation*, New York: Cambridge University Press.

Holpp, L. (1989) "Ten Reasons Why Total Quality is Less than Total," *Training* 26 (10): 93–103.

House, C. H. and Price, R. L. (1991) "The Return Map: Tracking Product Teams," *Harvard Business Review* 91 (Jan–Feb): 92–101.

Hunt, V. D. (1993) *Managing Quality: Integrating Quality and Business Strategy*, Homewood, IL: Irwin.

Ibara, H. (1992) "Structural Alignments, Individual Strategies, and Managerial Action: Elements Towards a Network Theory of Getting Things Done," in Nohria, N. and Eccles, R. G. (eds) *Networks and Organisations*.

Ishikawa, K. (1985) *What is Total Quality Control?*, Englewood Cliffs, NJ: Prentice Hall.

Juran, J. M. (1991) "Strategies for World-Class Quality," *Quality Progress* 24 (March): 81–85.

Juran, J. and Gryna, F. M. (1993) *Quality Planning and Analysis*, Singapore: McGraw Hill.

Kanter, R. M. (1984) *The Change Masters: Corporate Entrepreneurs at Work*, London: Routledge.

Kanter, R. M. (1988) "When a Thousand Flowers Bloom: Structural, Collective and Social Conditions for Innovation in Organisations," *Research in Organisational Behaviour* 10: 169–211.

Kaplan, R. E. (1984) "Trade Routes: The Manager's Network of Relationships," *Organisational Dynamics* (Spring): 37–52.

Kaplan, R. S. and Norton, D. P. (1992) "The Balanced Scorecard," *Harvard Business Review* 10 (Jan–Feb): 71–79.

Kaplan, R. S. and Norton, D. P. (1993) "Putting the Balanced Scorecard to Work," *Harvard Business Review* 71 (Sept–Oct): 134–147.

Kaplan, R. S. and Norton, D. P. (1996) *The Balanced Scorecard: Translating Strategy into Action*, Boston: Harvard Business School Press.

Kauffman, S. A. (1993) *The Origins of Order*, New York: Oxford University Press.

Kauffman, S. A. (1995) *At Home in the Universe*, London: Viking.

Kilmann, R. H. and Kilmann, I. (1991) *Making Organisations Competitive: Enhancing Networks and Relationships across Traditional Boundaries*, San Francisco: Jossey-Bass.

Kotter, J.P. (1982) "What Effective General Managers Really Do," *Harvard Business Review* 37: 156–167.

Krackhardt, D. (1990) "Assessing the Political Landscape: Structure, Cognition and Power in Organisations," *Administrative Science Quarterly* 35: 342–369.

Lave, J. and Wenger, E. (1994) *Situated Learning: Legitimate Peripheral Participation*, New York: Cambridge University Press.

Lehman Brothers (1994) *Pharma Pipelines*, London: Lehman Brothers.

Lindblom, L. (1959) "The Science of Muddling Through," *Public Administration Review* 19: 79–88.

Lipnack, J. and Stamps, J. (1993) "Networking the World: People, Corporations, Communities, and Nations," *Futurist* 27 (4): 9–12.

McManus, M. L. and Hergert, M. L. (1988) *Surviving Merger and Acquisition*, Glenview, IL: Scott Foresman.

McMillen, N. (1991) *Statistical Process Control and Company-Wide Quality Improvement*, London: IFS Publications.

McNeil, R. (1996) *Pharmaceutical Strategies: Class Acts*, London: FT Pharmaceuticals & Healthcare Publishing.

Mainzer, K. (1996) *Thinking in Complexity*, Heidelberg: Springer-Verlag.

March, J. G. and Olsen, J. P. (1976) *Ambiguity and Choice in Organisations*, Bergen, Norway: Universitetsforlaget.

Marion, R. (1999) *The Edge of Organization: Chaos and Complexity Theories of Formal Social Systems*, Thousand Oaks, CA: Sage Publications.

Marks, M. L. (1982) "Merging Human Resources," *Mergers and Acquisitions* 17 (2): 38–43.

Marsden, P. V. (1982) "Brokerage Behaviour in Restricted Exchange Networks," in Marsden, P. V. and Lin, N. (eds) *Social Structure and Network Analysis*, Beverly Hills: Sage.

Matthews, J. and Katel, P. (1992) "The Cost of Quality," *Newsweek* 120 (1): 48–49.

Mayo, E. (1933) *The Human Problems of an Industrialised Civilisation*, New York: Macmillan.

Mead, G. H. (1970) *Mind, Self and Society*, Chicago: University of Chicago Press.

Menzies-Lyth, I. (1988) *Containing Anxiety in Institutions*, London: Free Association Books.

Michael, J. and Yukl, G. (1993) "Managerial Level and Subunit Function as Determinants of Networking Behaviour in Organisations," *Group and Organisation Management* 18 (3): 328–351.

Mintzberg, H. (1973) *The Nature of Managerial Work*, New York: Harper & Row.

Mintzberg, H. (1994) *The Rise and Fall of Strategic Planning*, Hemel Hempstead: Prentice Hall.

Mintzberg, H. and Waters, J. A. (1985) "Of Strategies Deliberate and Emergent," *Strategic Management Journal* 6: 257–272.

Mirvis, P. H. (1985) "Negotiations after the Sale: The Roots and Ramifications of Conflict in an Acquisition," *Journal of Occupational Behaviour* 6 (1): 65–84.

Monge, P. R. and Eisenberg, R. M. (1987) "Emergent Communication Networks," in Jablin, F. M., Putnam, L. L., Roberts K. H. and Porter, L. W. (eds) *Handbook of Organisational Communication: An Interdisciplinary Perspective*, Beverly Hills: Sage.

Motsika, P. and Shalliff, K. (1990) "Ten Precepts Of Quality," *Quality Progress* 23 (Feb): 27–28.

Mueller, R. K. (1986) *Corporate Networking: Building Channels for Information and Influence*, New York: Free Press.

Myers, S. and Marquis, D. G. (1969) *Successful Industrial Innovation*, Washington, DC: National Science Foundation.

Napier, N. (1989) "Mergers and Acquisitions, Human Resource Issues and Outcomes: A Review and Suggested Typology," *Journal of Management Studies* 26 (3): 271–289.

Neave, H. R. (1990) *The Deming Dimension*, Knoxville, TN: SPC Press.

Nichols, N. A. (1994) "Scientific Management at Merck," *Harvard Business Review* 72 (Jan–Feb): 89–99.

Nohria, N. and Eccles, R. G. (1992) *Networks and Organisations*, Boston: Harvard Business School Press.

Numeroff, R. E. (1992) "How to Avoid Failure when Implementing a Quality Effort," *Tapping the Network Journal* 3 (4): 1–14.

Olian, J. D. and Rynes, S. L. (1991) "Making Total Quality Work: Aligning Organisations, Performance Measures, and Stakeholders," *Human Resource Management* 30: 303–333.

Orton, J. D. and Weick, K. (1990) "Loosely Coupled Systems: A Reconceptualisation," *Academy of Management Review* 15 (2): 203–223.

Ozbekhan, H. (1969) "Toward a General Theory of Planning," in Jantsch, E. (ed.) *Perspectives of Planning*, Paris: OECD.

Perry, L. T. (1986) "Merging Successfully: Sending the 'Right' Signals," *Sloan Management Review* 27 (3): 47–57.

Pfeffer, J. and Salancik, G. R. (1978) *The External Control of Organisations: A Resource Dependence Perspective*, New York: Harper & Row.

Pherson, H. G. (1994) "Give It Time," *Healthcare Forum* 37 (4): 34–38.

Poirier, C. C. and Reiter, S. E. (1996) *Supply Chain Optimisation: Building the Strongest Total Business Network*, San Francisco: Berrett-Koehler.

Price, F. (1989) "Out of Bedlam: Management by Quality Leadership," *Management Decision* 27: 15–21.

Prigogine, I. (1997) *The End of Certainty*, New York: Free Press.

Prigogine, I. and Stengers, I. (1985) *Order Out of Chaos*, London: Flamingo.

Quinn, J. J. (1996) "The Role of 'Good Conversation' in Strategic Control," *Journal of Management Studies* 33 (3): 381–394.

Reekie, W. D. (1975) *The Economics of the Pharmaceutical Industry*, London: Macmillan.

Roethlisberger, F. J. and Dickson, W. J. (1939) *Management and the Worker*, Boston: Harvard University Press.

Ross, D. F. (1998) *Competing Through the Supply Chain*, New York: Chapman & Hall.

Rothwell, R. (1992) "Successful Industrial Innovation: Critical Factors for the 1990s," *R&D Management* 22 (3): 221–239.

Scholtes, P. R. (1992) *The Team Handbook*, Madison, WI: Staruss Printing.

Schonberger, R. J. (1994) "Human Resource Management Lessons from a Decade of Total Quality Management and Reengineering," *California Management Review* 36 (Summer): 109–123.

Schwartzmann, D. (1976) *Innovation in the Pharmaceutical Industry*, Baltimore: Johns Hopkins University Press.

Schweiger, D. M., Ivancevich, J. M. and Power, F. R. (1987) "Executive Actions for Managing Human Resources Before and After Acquisition," *Academy of Management Executive* 1 (2): 127–138.

SG Warburg (1988) *DJIA: 2079.13*, New York: SG Warburg.

Shirley, R. C. (1977) "The Human Side of Merger Planning," *Long Range Planning* 10 (4): 35–39.

Shotter, J. (1994) *Conversational Realities*, London: Sage.

Shrader, C. B., Lincoln, J. R. and Hoffman, A. N. (1989) "The Network Structures of Organisations: Effects of Task Contingencies and Distributional Form," *Human Relations* 42: 43–66.

Slater, R. H. (1991) "Integrated Process Management: A Quality Model," *Quality Progress* 24 (Apr): 69–73.

Soin, S. S. (1992) *Total Quality Essentials: Key Elements, Methodologies, and Managing for Success*, New York: McGraw Hill.

Spencer, B. A. (1994) "Models of Organisation and Total Quality Management: A Comparison and Critical Evaluation," *Academy of Management Review* 19 (3): 446–471.

Stacey, R. (1996) *Complexity and Creativity in Organisations*, San Francisco: Berrett-Koehler Publications Inc.

Stacey, R. (2000) *Strategic Management and Organizational Dynamics: The Challenge of Complexity*, London: Pearson Education.

Stacey, R. (2001) *Complex Responsive Processes in Organizations: Learning and Knowledge Creation*, London: Routledge.

Stacey, R., Griffin, D. and Shaw, P. (2000) *Complexity and Management: Fad or Radical Challenge to Systems Thinking?*, London: Routledge.

Stewart, G. B. (1991) *The Quest For Value*, New York: Harper Collins.

Teltman, R. (1989) "Oh Henry!" *Financial World* (March): 30–32.

Tichy, N. (1981) "Networks in Organisations," in Nystrom, P. C. and Starbuck, W. H. (eds) *Handbook of Organisational Design*, vol. 2, New York: Oxford University Press.

Tichy, N. M. and Sherman, S. (1995) *Control Your Own Destiny or Someone Else Will*, London: HarperCollins Business.

Tillich, P. (1952) *The Courage to Be*, New Haven: Yale University Press.

Utterback, J. M. (1975) *The Process of Innovation in Five Industries in Europe and Japan*, New York: Centre For Policy Studies.

Van de Ven, A. H. (1988) "Central Problems in the Management of Innovation," in Tushman, M. L. and Moore, W. L. (eds) *Readings in the Management of Innovation*, New York: Harper.

Van Maanen, J. (1988) *Tales of the Field*, Chicago: University of Chicago Press.

Weber, J. (1991) "Merck Needs More Gold from the White Coats," *Business Week*, March 18: 58–60.

Webster's Encyclopaedic Unabridged Dictionary (1989) New York: Portland House.

Weick, K. (1979) *The Social Psychology of Organising*, Reading, MA: Addison-Wesley.

Weick, K. (1995) *Sensemaking in Organisations*, USA: Sage.

Wheelwright, S. C. and Clark, K. B. (1992) *Revolutionising Product Development: Quantum Leaps in Speed, Efficiency, and Quality*, New York: Maxwell Macmillan.

Wishard, B. J. (1985) "Merger – The Human Dimension," *Bank Administration* 61 (6): 74–79.

Wright, S. (1931) "Evolution in Mendelian Populations," *Genetics* 16: 97.

Zirger, B. and Maidique, M. (1990) "A Model of New Product Development: An Empirical Test," *Management Science* 36: 867–883.

Index